Revival
Surviving 100 Days

Revival
Surviving 100 Days

BASED ON A TRUE STORY

E L I S E   M I C O M Y I Z A

REVIVAL
Surviving 100 Days

Published by Elise Micomyiza, Edmonton, Canada

ISBN:
    Paperback   978-1-77354-564-6
       ebook   978-1-77354-565-3

Publication assistance by

PAGEMASTER
PUBLISHING
PageMaster.ca

Dedication

To my amazing mother Byukusenge, my father Micomyiza who departed too soon, my siblings Diane and Zoro who I couldn't shield, my younger siblings, my lovely children Micaela and Mico who brighten my days, my supportive husband John who encouraged me to chase my dreams. I also want to acknowledge Imfura Loiic, my friends and family who stood by me through thick and thin. And to Shangazi, who endured great loss yet continued to smile, love unconditionally, and never blamed the world for all that it has taken from her.

Contents

Prologue

March 31, 1994, at 6:20 p.m.

"Bring me another bottle and two more for these men!" A man in khaki pants shouted to the bartender, a woman with sagging breasts and badly bleached skin. She looked at the man with contempt in her eyes, but she did as he instructed. The small bar reeked of an unpleasant mixture of alcoholic beverages, *urwagwa*, local beer, primus, chief waragi, and a mixture of grilled meats. The people in the bar didn't seem to mind, though.

The three men sat there discussing, with their obvious lecherous gaze, the woman who was searching, bending over to pick up a bottle of beer from the crate. She either didn't care or she cared too much. When she returned to the table, holding the beers close to her chest, and put them on the table, the men smiled. The one in Khaki pants smiled back and licked his scarred pouty lips.

"Here is your hot beer." She said it in a high-pitched voice. She proceeded to open other beers for the two men. The dim lighting in the bar illuminated her bleached skin and made the persistent black spots even more visible. Either the men didn't care or they were into her black spots on the temple, her knuckles, and her ankles.

"Does anyone want to get some meat with this beer, though? I could particularly use a hot brochette and a good woman with curves in the right places." The man in khaki pants slapped her butt, and others laughed. The woman winced but smiled broadly, as if she were used to being treated like this every single day.

"I agree with you. We can take some brochette; business has been going well enough for us to afford one. If you're really lucky, you will get a trial with her." Another man with a thick afro sitting on top of his head said. The woman turned her attention to her and smiled at him seductively, as if she would prefer him over his scarred, pouty-lipped friend.

"Alright, get us two brochettes each. Those are six. Bring them while they're still hot. Put ten potatoes on the grill for us too." The man in Khaki said. "And don't just stay there; come and have a beer with us, *Cherie*!"

The woman faked a shy grin and moved away, her gait a bit more exaggerated.

"I love how fast you are!" The afro-man laughed and gave his friend a firm handshake that reverberated in the small bar on impact.

The third man, who was potbellied and silent throughout the ordeal, shook his head and commented, "Your wife must be very depressed."

"No, she has children to keep her company at home. I need to always test younger women to stay healthy." The man in khaki pants refuted.

"Haha, alright. Let's hope it doesn't get to your wife." The afro haired man replied.

"How would she know? I left her in Ruhengeri. Who is going to tell her that I was here testing women in Kigali?" The man in Khaki said.

"You know what they say; even the walls have ears, you can never be sure who is listening." The pot bellied man retorted.

As they spoke, another relatively taller man came from behind their table and called out.

"Lando, Matthieu, and Kalisa!" The man exclaimed. "I didn't know that I was going to find you three here. Who knew that Lando also came to the city? I thought you would be searching for money in Ruhengeri only!"

Lando, the man in khaki pants, looked at the man, not so pleased with the familiarity obviously, but he kept his expression in check and responded half-heartedly, "Ha, I can't leave the city to you and Matthieu and Kalisa; I came to see what you've got too!"

Matthieu, the afro-haired man, stood up and greeted the taller man, "Gasana! I wasn't expecting you either; I had heard you went again to Uganda for business; when did you come back?"

"Oh, I just came back last night. I was spending some days in Ruhengeri as well, checking on the prices of the products there. It has been hard to get good prices here. I was checking on how the business environment is to see if I can expand there. I even went to check on Lando, but I learned that he was in Kigali instead. It's a good thing that we just met here." Gasana said.

The pot-bellied man, Kalisa, busied himself with getting a chair from another empty table and made space for Gasana to sit.

"It's always good to be with businessmen; you haven't even sat down, but you're already talking about projects!" Kalisa said.

He seemed as cheerless as Lando about Gasana's arrival, but they both simply accommodated him.

Lando called on the woman to get Gasana a beer. When the woman arrived, she seemed to be transfixed with Gasana instead of Lando, who had called.

"So what can I get you?" She cooed.

"Just a primus will be good for me." Gasana said as he adjusted into the plastic chair and let out a long sigh. The woman stood there,Gasana, looking at him.

"We just ordered some brochettes as well. Let her know if they can put on more for you too." Matthieu told Gasana who quickly said that they could add two for him as well.

Finally, when the woman left, Lando followed her with his gaze again and the men laughed and filled in Gasana.

"Lando has caught one fresh fish here!" Kalisa said.

Amused, Gasana said, "I don't know about it being a fresh fish, but obviously it is an available fish."

"Don't listen to those men. They're so stuck with their old, wrinkled wives that they don't want to try out new things. It's such a woman who is experienced that she can satisfy a man. Our women are busy tending to the households, bearing children, and raising them; they don't have time to really learn about pleasing a man!" Lando explained to the men who sipped their beers and shook their heads at his philosophy.

"I can understand that once in a while, one needs to try something new, but Lando, you try everywhere, in every village!" Kalisa exclaimed and the men laughed again.

"I don't need to try new things. My wife surprises me every time, and I am more than satisfied with her." Gasana said in a serious tone, but the others just laughed.

"Sometimes I wonder if that wife of yours has not poisoned you or cast a spell on you. You need to be a real man, Gasana; you cannot be attached to the hems of her skirts for the rest of your life. When you start doing business with me, I will show you how it is done." Lando said.

"Speaking of business, we heard that it is going very well for you, the bill is yours tonight, haha!" Kalisa said with obvious mockery in his voice.

"You people are now becoming boring; as someone who works in the hospital, do you think I understand all those business talks of yours? Let's just put on some music; we can't drink, eat, and not dance." Matthieu complained.

As they spoke, the woman came with the plates of brochette and went back again to bring plates with potatoes. The aroma spread into the small bar, and the men licked their lips in anticipation.

"They're smelling the right way! I like their way of grilling meat, for sure. Give us another round of beer!" Lando said, pulling his chair towards the table. "Let's dig in!"

As each of the men picked up a skewer, Matthieu complained again, "There is no radio to be found in this place or something?" He called out to the woman, who said that she would see what she could do. In a few minutes, she returned with a Sonitec radio, placed it on the dirty, cemented floor of the bar, and switched it on. "Search for the station with music."

Before she could start tuning, Lando said, "I just remembered that there could be some news at this time. Wait a bit; we'll do it for ourselves, Cherie. Thank you. Though I wanted you to join us, you did not. I can see you have more clients, but don't forget about me!" He winked at the woman, who faked a shy smile again. She walked away and left the men at the table. However, the radio presenter's voice took over, and they all halted.

Hinga mpere ku matangazo yo kubika, amatangazo yo kubika, ku butumwa bwanyu ku bagize ibyago (Let me start with death announcements, obituaries, and your notices to those who had mishaps.)

The family of Rucakatsi Tomas in Ruhengeri is saddened to inform family and friends that his son, Ingabire Alphonse Katumba, passed away last night due to bandit attacks. The family announces that the funeral is tomorrow, April 1, 1994, in Commune Kigombe in Ruhengeri at Gashangiro. This family also informs those in Secteur Muhungwe Commune Karago and those in Nkuri, to reach out in haste. The body will be buried at 11 am.

After the obituary, Matthieu took the initiative and switched off the radio hurriedly. The men looked at one another warily without speaking, the air thick with tension and suspicion. Lando and Kalisa looked at Gasana sinisterly. Matthieu was the one to break the silence, and fill in. "These brochettes are very tasty!" None of the men responded.

Suddenly, Lando stood up, picked up the beer in a half-empty glass, and threw it on Gasana. Gasana stood up, wondering what just happened.

"Why would you pour a glass of beer on me?" Gasana inquired, wiping the beer from his face. Just then, Kalisa threw more on his torso, drenching him in the beer.

Matthieu also stood in alarm and pleaded with Lando and Kalisa. "I don't know what the issue is, but we shouldn't settle it like this. We don't need to embarrass ourselves in a bar like this. All of you are powerful men."

"I still don't understand why you would do this to me! We were supposed to be talking about business now." Gasana asked the two men, who laughed at him.

"Do business with you? Do you think I don't know what your business is? You're a spy!" Lando said in an ominous tone as he picked up an empty bottle from the table.

"I don't know what you're talking about!" Gasana shouted at him as he winced at his drenched shirt and pants.

"Deny it all you want, all cockroaches are the same! You're all snakes, and it is time we beat you to death!" Kalisa retorted at Gasana, whose eyes filled with fear.

"I don't think he even knew that Katumba was dying! Let's not blame someone who doesn't have anything to do with those political things. How would he know? Gasana is just a harmless businessman." Matthieu reasoned.

"So you want to cooperate with him as well? Or you're also one of the spies?" Lando said and turned to Matthieu, who raised his palms midair in surrender.

"At first you killed Bucyana, then Mutombo, then Leone, so now it's Katumba?" Lando shrieked. "I hope you know that one day it will be you, that bag of bones you call a wife, and those kids of yours."

Gasana's eyes widened in fear, Kalisa picked up a second bottle and approached Gasana, who was trying as hard as he could to wipe the beer off his face and clothes.

"We are fed up with your snobbish behavior towards our people. You're snakes, but you will no longer continue to spread your venom because we have already prepared. You don't understand just how much I hate you. You have been pretending to do business, but we know you're a spy on your fellow snakes. I am telling you now, to your face, that we hate you. Take it however you want. One more person will die, and I will personally burn you and your family until nothing can be seen but ashes!" Kalisa exploded into a rant that made trepidation manifest on Gasana's face.

Realizing what was going on, he backed off, eyeing the three men in front of him. Lando and Kalisa were ready to smash the bottles on his head, probably, and there was Matthieu, who stood there spellbound by the whole ordeal. The atmosphere was thick with hatred, fear, and something more sinister and dangerous, death. Gasana could feel sweat run down his spine as if he had run a marathon.

In the heat of the moment, he picked up his own bottle from the table, still full of beer as he hadn't drunk much of it, and bolted out of the small bar. Mucoma, the griller, the woman, and a few other people in the corners of the bar were watching, but none dared to ask questions or act alarmed. It was as if they understood what Lando and Kalisa were talking about. If they didn't, they just didn't want to stir trouble.

Gasana had bolted out of the bar, drenched in the beer, running with a beer bottle that was spilling all the way as he ran. His mind was fixed on his beautiful home, his courageous wife, who had given him four healthy, intelligent children, and everything that they had built together. With every step as he ran, crossing the main road and entering the dirt road that led to his house, his eyes could not see where he was really running, but his heart knew. His heart beats for his home. He could not bear to lose them. Dust filled his nostrils as he breathed heavily and ran with the bottle. In ten minutes, he was at the gate of his house.

The dog barked in alarm as he stormed in, it almost attacked him, but it recognized him. He closed the gate with a bar of steel bent to form a U. As he got into the house, everyone else was engrossed in something playing on the television, but his wife and eight-year-old daughter, Anne, came outside. He sat on the steps, catching his breath.

"Darling, what happened? You're soaked in beer!" Mama Anne queried, looking perplexed as Anne stood there watching her father, who was soaked and silent.

"I don't know; you know what? Start packing!" Gasana said, his voice shaking with terror.

"What are you talking about? Anne, go sit with others in the living room. I am coming." Mama Anne said.

"Honey, you don't understand; they want to kill me; they want to kill us. They're going to burn us alive. There is no way that we are going to stay here." Gasana vented.

"You're really not making sense. You need to calm down first. I think you need to remove those clothes first and take a bath; Donatha has already prepared the hot water for you." Mama Anne pleaded with Gasana, who seemed to not hear a word.

"I don't want to lose you or my children. You're the blessing I have in this life and beyond. All I want is to see you all safe. Do you understand me? Please understand me. I want you to listen to me. Go and pack the bags. Now!" Gasana yelled, tears flowing down his face. His wife realized that something wasn't right. Gasana was not a weakling of a man. He was not a coward. He was one of the strongest people she knew. He would move hell and earth for her. Despite fifteen years of marriage, his love has been as steady as it was when they met twenty years ago.

They had always been one another's best friend and advisor, through thick and thin. She was there when he had nothing. They had built a business and a home together. In all these years, she had never seen him this afraid.

She sat down next to him on the cemented steps of their house and calmly touched his forearm.

"Darling, alright, I am going to pack the bags as you say. But it is late. I also need to know what I will tell our children when they ask me why we are doing this. It's been a long time since they came to search for you. It was two years ago, remember? Recently, it's been just rumors. It's just your rivals who don't want to see you prosper; they want you to waver and lose your path. Dear, we're not politicians; we have never been involved in politics before; it's just the rumors." She said, trying to calm him down.

"I don't think you understand. Do you think it's a joke when they do this to me? I am well respected, but Kalisa and Lando dared to pour beer on me. What do you think is next?" Gasana asked his wife, looking at her.

In that moment, as their eyes held. He took a deep breath and calmed down a bit, replying to his wife's silent plea, he told her the story of what happened at the bar.

"Another big person in the CDR died, Katumba is dead." He said, "They have been suspecting me since a long time ago. It is hard for me to remain calm when they threaten to kill you and our children. Money is not an issue for me, but you already know that the hatred they have for us runs deeper than their greed. I know these men."

"Alright. So what do you think we should do?" Mama Anne asked, realizing that the matter was much more complex than she had anticipated. She had been thinking that it was the same as the usual threats.

"That's what I was trying to tell you!"

"Yes, repeat, a little bit calmer, or you're going to alert the children too." Gasana realized that his wife had a point there.

"We're going to take all the children to Ndekezi's house at Deutsche Welle. We'll take only Donatha, the other housekeeper will stay here, and the house guard will stay here. We'll hide there for a few days while I figure out how to send the children to my sisters' in Ruhengeri." Gasana illustrated.

"Alright, that's a good plan. I hope you can find a way to send the children maybe tomorrow instead of taking them with us to Deutsche Welle." Mama Anne said.

After a back and forth of what they could do, the couple arrived at a consensus of sending all the older children—the older brother of fifteen, the next of twelve, and another of ten—and remaining with their only daughter, Anne. Gasana went ahead and took the bath, and he made his best effort to appear as cheerful as possible as he announced to the children that they would go visit his sister's home the next day. They questioned their father's decision to visit over a school period, and he explained that there would be an event at his sister's house.

Gasana had done his best to bring up his children comfortably. They fed on the best meals, prepared by Donatha, who had studied cooking; they always got the best technologies coming up; they played the best games; and he made sure to show them around on the regular trips they had. However, he also made sure that they learned the basic necessities of life, such as cleaning up after themselves, despite the fact that they had workers.

At home, they spoke mostly French and read French books, but discussed in Kinyarwanda whenever there were serious matters to speak about. He had also made sure that they had the basics in English, as his business was mostly in Uganda. He wanted them to understand his trade so they could take over.

Thinking about how two men had threatened to make his years of building a powerful family perish in vain made Gasana's mind boggle.

As they went to sleep, Gasana could not stop turning around in bed. He didn't feel safe despite having a home protected by a trained home guard, a dog, barbed wires around the brick fence, and the best locks on the house.

"I think you need to sleep and try to forget those mad men's antics." His wife said as she kissed his cheek in the dark, wrapped her arms around his torso, and went to sleep.

The next day, he made sure that the three older boys packed their things in the suitcases and loaded them in the white van they mostly used for trips, and they left. He sighed as he stood with his wife and daughter at the gate, watching the van rev away through the dusty road.

He also planned to set out for Deutsche Welle. He noticed that his home guard, who was also in charge of cleaning his personal car, had not cleaned it since he had parked it.

"Zamu, why did you not wash my car?" Gasana asked, baffled. In their three years of working together, Zamu had not been a disobedient subject. Despite his frequent drinking problems whenever he got his salary, he seemed like an agreeable person who did what he was asked to do.

"I just have too much work to do today." Zamu said unapologetically as he continued watering the garden that didn't look like it needed to be watered at 10 a.m.

"Use only fifteen minutes to dust it at least; I am in a hurry." Gasana said. He hated being late for anything. He always liked to be on time, but people also associated it with him behaving like a white person or as if he was more important than the others.

"What's the point of dusting it? You're going to drive in the dust again!" Zamu replied in a disrespectful tone that he had not used with his employer before. Gasana realized this, but he decided that he would deal with his employee when the imperative issues had passed.

"Just do as I said."

With that, he went back inside to prepare for their departure with his wife and daughter.

At Deutsche Welle, they only spent two days, and Gasana decided that the rumors of him being a spy that led to the death of Katumba had died out. They all returned home, but he decided that his other children could remain at his sister's for a few more days.

Unbeknownst to Gasana and his family, the genocide that would turn their world upside down was lurking around the corner.

Part 1: The Storm

Chapter 1

The few days that Gasana had spent in the place where he had fled to, Kinyinya, he could not sleep. Sleep was something he chased all night, and while it was running in the streets without a care, he had distractions—unpleasant distractions. He could not help but think about his sister and the three boys that he had sent there, in hopes that they would be safe with his sister. She had married a Hutu man in the north, hoping that she would get a safer life and that her children would not be discriminated against within the school settings like his were.

Gasana had stayed in Kinyinya since April 1, and they returned the morning of April 3. He followed the news every day, trying to make sure that no one else died, and he was blamed for it. He was very afraid of what would become of him and his family. He had tried to keep his children from encountering the harsh reality that every other Tutsi had to face in life. He had grown up with a family that loved him and introduced him to everything he needed to become the successful businessman that he was. He was respected wherever he went, and there was a ghastly edge when other businessmen spoke of him. They knew that he was capable of doing more than he let on.

He had been blessed with a feisty wife who was as creative and courageous as she was breathtaking. There was no one else he would have chosen to spend the rest of his life with. She was a woman who kept him on his toes despite the distance. Almost all the business ventures that he had were inspired by their pillow talks. She was a woman who made the home cozy and homely, but when it was time to discuss money, she spoke up dauntlessly. He had spent his days in Kinyinya talking to her, eating with her, and spending time with their daughter. Gasana realized that he missed his family time, which had shrunk with his lengthy business trips in East Africa.

His daughter, an eight-year-old bundle of joy with bob hair braids with bright and colorful beads, was the apple of his eye. He liked his children, but this was his princess. He wished she would live as long as possible until she got married and had children of her own. She was very smart, like her mother, and she carried both of their features. Prominent cheekbones like her mother, his own voluminous hair, and many other traits While their boys were born with one parent's features, the lovely girl was a living reminder of how blissful his marriage was. He had had to counsel a lot of his agemates who had gotten bored after a number of years and started to stray in their marriages. They claimed that their wives had stopped being their enthusiastic, bubbly selves, and they needed to find fresh girls who could serve them with their youthful bodies and shy smiles. He asked them if they were their energetic and doting boys; they had been back when their wives were girls, and their responses would be 'no, but men never get old.'

Gasana loved his wife in all the colors possible. He loved her for the commitment she had to him. He loved her for choosing him to spend their lives together, growing together. The wrinkles she had accumulated over the years were more beautiful than the youthful bodies of women she saw in different bars and clubs. They were memories of how fortunate he had been. They reminded him of her patience in carrying and raising three boys on most occasions, given that he was mostly on business trips and such. He respected her for that. He deemed every man who didn't respect their wives for such trifling issues a weak man who had no ethical thinking. He could not claim that they had never had fights because, with a spirit like hers, his wife was not an agreeable woman. She was very assertive, and she would not do anything for the sake of doing it. He often found himself tired of discussing business matters with her. However, he loved that it was challenging; one cannot give fully understandable details unless they understand the matter themselves. The questioning she gave him about his businesses would have been considered nagging by most men, but he was grateful, for it had saved him a lot of money that he could have lost.

On April 3, he was back at home, sitting on the porch, reading a book. He was a committed Catholic alongside his family, but amid the whole ordeal and fleeing, they all didn't have the energy to really go through with going to church and preparing the parties that they used to host at his home. This time, it was a calm Easter time without children visiting his own children and playing in the backyard, without the families gathering and popping sounds of beer bottles, and without the delicious aroma of his wife's food.

He watched his guard wash slowly with a small radio snuggled in the crease of his shoulder and head. Gasana couldn't help but notice that the guard that he has been with for a couple of years has been changing a lot. He had asked Zamu to dust his car before they left, and his impertinent attitude irked Gasana a lot. He wasn't an unbearable employer; he always understood and factored in that everyone can have their bad days. Maybe Zamu was having a bad day as well. However, at this point, he had no doubt that the guard was onto something. One does not disrespect their employers unless they want to find a reason to leave employment or are about to betray their masters. He hoped it wasn't the latter.

"Hi Darling, Are you listening to the news?" His wife called from behind him, carrying a jug of juice with the two cups.

"Hi honey, no, I am not; I was just reading a book. Why?" Gasana asked his wife. Who said nothing but sat down on the chair beside him and busied herself with pouring the juice for the two of them?

"On RTLM…" His wife started.

"Honey, listen, you need to stop listening to that stupid radio. You can at least watch television if you really need something to entertain you. That radio does nothing but spread nonsensical ideas." Gasana said. He couldn't really tell if he really said it out of concern for his wife or out of distress about what his wife had heard exactly.

"You keep saying that, but remember what happened the last time you heard news on that radio?"

"What? Just because these crazy men decided to trash me in public, I can't just live in fear that they would do it again because of just radio presenters. They could have been just too drunk." Gasana retorted. "God is on our side; His will dictates our lives. We can't behave like non-believers!"

He knew that panic had crept into his system that day. He was on the edge; he felt like something dreadful was going to happen, but he didn't want his wife to be afraid as well. He was the man of the house, and he would do as he had been groomed to be: a protector of the family.

"The same radio presenters are now onto something worse than just informing, though. They're not saying that RPF is going to do something, but they won't be seated. They'll fight back. I am no political expert, but it doesn't take a genius to know that something wrong is about to happen." His wife said, handing him the juice after noticing that he wasn't picking up the cup.

"Hey, listen. Nothing wrong will happen. Even if it does, we have money. We have been blessed to have worked all these years to be comfortable. Most of the people who can harm us will be looking for money. I have money, properties, and businesses. They'll save us in difficult times." Gasana reassured his wife, who gave him an incredulous look.

"I can only hope that you're right." Mama Anne said, and she gulped the remainder of her juice as she looked at Zamu, who was still washing the car with one hand and another holding the radio. "I don't know if it's me or if he has been changing. He is less obedient than he was. Donatha mentioned that he has been behaving weirdly since the day that we left until now."

"Maybe he has worked for enough money, and he's looking for reasons to be fired. It happens." Gasana said to his wife.

"I don't believe it is that simple. There could be something else. Right after the incident at the bar, that's when he started behaving weirdly. Don't you think those two are connected, maybe?" Mama Anne probed.

"I think you're making a hill out of a molehill. Don't you remember that this is not the first time this has happened? This is a common thing among houseworkers; sometimes they can tell that you're not planning to fire them at all, and they try to find reasons as to why you should let them go. Not because of you, but for their own reasons." Gasana replied. He knew deep in his heart that his wife could be having a point, but his brain was already filled with dread; he didn't want to add to it.

"Trust me, we're better safe than sorry. I think we should fire him right away. I no longer trust him." Mama Anne said, looking at her husband intently.

"Don't worry. I will think about it more. Call my daughter here. Even though we are in trouble, I really enjoyed my time hanging out with the both of you. Maybe later on we'll play some cards and watch television. It's Sunday; my business partner might show up later in the evening bringing some papers and some money that he owes me." Gasana elaborated.

"Alright, dear, I'll be with Donatha in the kitchen; I haven't finished making the juice. Let me check on her." Mama Anne said She picked up the empty cups and jug and went back inside.

Even though Gasana had been trying to put on a tough front, he knew that his wife's suspicion could be true, and if it turned out to be true, he didn't really know what he'd do.

"Anne, Anne!" Gasana called out his daughter.

"Oui, papa!" Anne yelled from inside.

"Come out here! Daddy wants to tell you something. Bring your story books too!" Gasana shouted with a laughter-filled voice. His heart always brimmed with warmth whenever he thought about his daughter.

Anne came with her three storybooks, which were in three languages: English, French, and Kinyarwanda. Gasana wanted his children to learn languages from a young age to make sure that they would move through the world comfortably. However, unlike many rich people who seemed to hate the vernacular language with passion, he didn't hate his mother tongue. It was the language that allowed him to speak to his people; it was a language that brought out emotions in him. He wanted his children to carry it as a part of their legacy.

"Je suis là, papa!" Anne said as she stood in front of her father, who looked up at her with an adoring gaze.

"Let's speak in Kinyarwanda, okay?" Gasana said. "You speak French at school, so at home we speak in Kinyarwanda and English sometimes, alright?"

Anne nodded shyly and sat in the chair previously occupied by her mother.

"Did you get the juice from your mother?" Gasana queried, and that won him a cheerful grin from his daughter, whose teeth had just grown back in.

"Awesome! So tell me, how have you been today? What did you read?"

"I read different stories in the Kinyarwanda book. I read a lot of stories about Bakame, the Lion, and other animals. He was a very clever hare!" Anne said it with excitement. "I particularly like that he is very small but very intelligent to outsmart big and scary animals like the lion."

"Yes, I love that! It's just like how you're still a pretty little girl, but who is very intelligent and smart?" Gasana exclaimed.

He was a father who had never beaten a child of his own. While spanking and flogging children was a popular way of disciplining children, he had never done so. He believed that his children had the brains to really listen whenever he told them that something was bad. None of his children had really been troublemakers; while they all had their mother's fiery nature, they also had his reasonable mind. Whenever he prohibited them from doing something, he always gave them reasons as to why they should never do so. In return, they were very comfortable, even confessing their own mistakes and apologizing whenever they were in the wrong.

"Really? Papa, do you think I am really smart?" Anne asked, her eyes full of hope that her father would praise her intelligence. However, it was unlike Anne or any of his children to doubt their own intelligence. Gasana and his wife had always ensured that their children were not lacking in terms of compliments. Whenever they did something well, they were rewarded. Whenever they did something wrong, they made sure to reprimand them, but not harshly.

They had undisputable trust amongst them as a family. As his boys grew, he introduced them to what he did and how he had started his business. Sometimes they complained that he repeated those stories too much, but he knew that it was necessary. He wanted them to know the roots of his wealth. He wanted them to be strong men of both character and drive in life. He wanted them to be more than he ever was. Even though he wasn't a weakling, he wanted them to be wealthy and well-spoken men when they grew up. He could always see that his efforts were not in vain; they were already showing signs of success at an early age.

However, the thought of his daughter doubting herself shocked him. It wasn't usual. She was a very confident girl who never gave up on herself.

"Why do you ask, dear?" Gasana asked as he looked at Anne intently, and she looked down as she fiddled with her fingers. She wasn't a timid girl. She always expressed her thoughts, just like her mother. Unless when she was hurt or apologizing for her misdeeds.

"One child at school said that I am not smart and intelligent. She said that her parents said that I am a cockroach, and cockroaches can't, so I am not smart." Anne said, biting her lips to not cry.

Gasana was stunned for a minute. He didn't know what to say. As much as he tried to camouflage his children from the bitter truth of what it meant to be a Tutsi, he had no control over who they would meet. He gathered his thoughts to respond without giving his child the illusion that she was smarter than everyone else.

"Dear, you're not smart because I or any other person says you are. You're simply smart because you're you. It's in you. What's in you can never be taken away by anyone else. You're intelligent as a person. It doesn't matter what your colleagues say." He held her hands gently and asked, "Haven't you seen a cockroach before?"

"Yes, I saw one in the storeroom one day." Anne replied.

"Do you think you look like it?"

"No, I don't; they're very small, they climb on things, and they often hide in dark rooms." Anne responded.

"So, your colleague is wrong. Just ignore those comments. Maybe your colleague is very confused about cockroaches because they have not seen one yet." Gasana said. He knew what it meant, but he didn't want to introduce his child to such notions before she was at least ten years old.

"But Papa, even other children in my class agreed with her that I am a cockroach, along with Annabelle and Keza. They said that we are cockroaches and that they should step on us and kill us because that's what you do when you see a cockroach." Anne said. "Are they going to kill me, papa?"

Gasana realized that the issue was deeper than he had thought. He didn't understand why such young children had been introduced to such malicious ideology already. He wondered whether the school was actually safe for his daughter to go to or if he should just take her to school in Uganda or Kenya. Education there was of a high standard, and there was bearable insecurity. However, other than his business partners, he didn't have family from Kenya, apart from his sister Costa, who was also very busy as a widowed mother who ran multiple businesses up in Uganda to make ends meet.

"Anne, you're not a cockroach or any other animal that they will say you are; neither are Annabelle or Keza. All of you are beautiful children who will grow into wonderful women. Don't listen to what they say. Alright?" Gasana said it in a conclusive tone. At the moment, he didn't know how to approach this.

"Okay, papa. Will you protect me when they come to kill me?" Anne asked, on the verge of tears.

"I will always protect you. Your mother and your brother will also protect you." Gasana said that and hugged his daughter tight until she squirmed in discomfort.

"Sorry, darling, go back and read more of Bakame's stories, okay? When your brothers are back, you will tell them some of the tales too, alright?" Gasana instructed.

"Okay, Papa," Anne ran back inside. Gasana sat there, digesting what he had just learned. His fear was mounting with every interaction. He ran his hands in his well-trimmed, neat afro in thought, wondering what all these signs meant.

He thought about his businesses, which were in different places. He knew that he needed to reach out to his sister, Costa, and his other sister, Dorothea, who had his boys. Just in case something happened, they would know what to do. He wasn't a cheating businessman; he always paid what he owed and settled every account on time. He had enemies just like every other businessman, but it was mostly out of envy or competition, not hate. However, he was starting to feel hatred lurking around him.

In a few minutes, as he was lost deep in thought, Anne came back outside to the porch, holding the story book.

"Papa, I want to go visit Jeph. He visited me last Sunday, so I told him that I would return the favor too." Anne said.

"Anne, it's already 3 p.m. in the afternoon; don't you think it is better to visit him maybe another day?" Gasana said. It wasn't really about the visit. He no longer felt comfortable letting his daughter out of his sight. He was also going to write to call his sister in the north to bring back his sons.

"No, Papa, I promised him that I would not lie to him. Please let me visit him today, at least for an hour." Anne pleaded. She looked so adorable in her pink dress that he always found it hard to deny her anything.

"Are you sure you will only spend an hour there?" Gasana gave in. "If you don't come back after an hour, that will mean that we will remove those minutes from the time you spend at the playgrounds. Deal?"

"Okay, deal. Send Donatha in one hour, because I don't have a watch. I will immediately come when she asks for me at Jeph's house." Anne said.

She was a smart girl. Her intelligence and depth of character never ceased to amaze him, and he was always proud to say that he was the daughter of such an amazing girl. She just had a lot of older people's mannerisms at times that scared him. He wondered whether she was living the life that every young girl needs to live. She was a child who helped her mother in the kitchen, took initiative to clean things at the house even when no one asked her, and was always eager to learn something new.

"Alright, I'll tell her for sure. Have fun!" Gasana said as she watched her trot away.

***

Anne jogged to her friend's house. Jeph was a ten-year-old boy that she went to school with. Her parents and his parents were friends, and they visited one another. They had moved to the house next to theirs just recently, but they had bonded after two family visits. At Jeph's house, they had cute black and white-furred cats that they petted together when their parents had their grown-up talks.

They were both in the same grade at school, and they spent most of their time together at school. She liked that even though Jeph was not a Tutsi like her, he didn't call her a cockroach or say that she was not smart and intelligent. Jeph loved science and environment-related studies. They spent some time reading about plants and scientific concepts together.

While most of the children at her school spoke just French, Jeph was never afraid to speak Kinyarwanda and very little English that he knew. He also seemed interested in reading English storybooks with her.

Both of them always had fun together, regardless of where they were. This always surprised Anne as well because she had thought he would bond more with her brothers as they were peers, but he seemed to like her better. Even though he also played with her brothers, he didn't seem to be too fond of them.

As Anne reached Jeph's house, she didn't find anyone outside, so she knocked at their door three times. Her parents had always said that it was bad manners to knock more than three times. She didn't know why, but she kept on the manner. After a few minutes, their house help, a plump girl who spoke with a stammer, came to the door and greeted her.

"How are you, Anne?" she said. Anne had laughed behind her fist the first time she heard her speak, but Jeph had berated her, saying that it was mocking someone just because she couldn't speak as they did. From then on, Anne learned not to laugh at people who had disabilities of any sort.

"Hi Maria, I came to see Jeph." Anne said.

"He is inside watching television." Maria stuttered, "You can enter and see him."

Anne really liked that at Jeph's house everyone was treated with respect, and out of many other children that she went to school with, Jeph seemed to be the only one to think that their housemaid was also a human being. Others shared stories about how they never did anything for themselves because they had maids and how worthless their housemaids and house guards were.

Anne entered the house and let herself into the cozy living room, filled with many fun family photos of Jeph and his parents. The ones they had taken when he was baptized, the ones they took when he was in school at different events, and others that they had taken when he was a baby. Everything reflected love in their house. No wonder Jeph was such a good friend to her.

"Hi Jeph!" Anne exclaimed.

"Hi Anne," he responded, stopping the animated film he was watching. "You actually came!" They hugged lightly and sat together on the sofa.

"What are you watching?" Anne inquired.

"Just some animated film; I don't know the name; I found the CD just there." Jeph replied, "But it's actually good. When you didn't come at 1 p.m., I was thinking that you're no longer coming."

"No, I had some homework to do and books to read in the afternoon. I had to beg my father to let me come at this hour." Anne said.

"Hmm, you brought the English storybook that you talked about the other day." Jeph mused.

"Yes, this one is the easiest I have; my dad bought it for me when I was starting, so you can understand a few things for now." Anne explained.

"Alright." Jeph took the story book from her and put it on the table. "Do you want to eat a mango or a banana?"

"I just drank some juice at home before I came. I don't want anything now." Anne said. "Do you also think I am a cockroach that's not smart?"

"Who told you that? Don't tell me that you actually believe what Nusra told you the other day at school!" Jeph exclaimed in disbelief.

"No, but I also think there is a reason why she kept calling me a cockroach. Besides, I have heard it on the radio when Donatha is listening to the radio. When I ask her why, they say that she doesn't explain." Anne said, dispirited.

"Anne, you're not a cockroach or a snake; you're a human being. Donatha maybe didn't want you to think much about that nonsense." Jeph responded. "You should just ignore people like Nusra at school; maybe they got that from their housemaids."

"However much we are ignoring this, I think it is serious. I have also heard the house guard say that my parents are cockroaches when he was speaking to someone I didn't know at the gate." Anne said.

"You can't care about everything you hear, Anne; it is complicated." Jeph sighed.

"I know that we are not the same; your family is Hutu and we are Tutsi, but you don't seem to hate us as the other people do. Do you know that the other day, my father came back soaked in beer? He tried to keep it from us, but he sent my brothers to my aunts' place. We also went to another place called Kinyinya for, like, two days. Do you think some bad things are going to happen to us?" Anne said.

Jeph thought for a moment and replied, "I don't think so; maybe there is something going on in terms of business. My father also says that he has some enemies because he is successful in his business. He always tells me to be careful around some people. They're jealous. I think it is the same case with your father, maybe."

"I don't think so. Even my mother seemed to be afraid for the past few days."

"Anne, I think you should calm down. How about I bring some of the new toys that my father sent me from Belgium? He's going to be there for quite some time, so he decided to send them to me." Jeph proposed.

"From Belgium!" Anne exclaimed, "I'd love to see them. They must be very nice."

Jeph went ahead and brought the toys; a mere thirty minutes later, the conversation seemed to be as if it didn't happen as they played with different toys, read stories, and shared gossip from their school. When the time was up, Donatha came to take Anne home. However, to her misery, the few next days on April 6, she learned from her parents that Jeph and his mother relocated to join his father in Belgium. She didn't know whom she was going to be talking to about the tension that had been building up in her family house. Her mother and father had been looking very afraid of something for a couple of days. Her brothers were still at their aunt's place, and she was feeling very lonely and scared.

Little did she know that the disaster that would dismantle their loving family was mere hours away.

Chapter 2

Gasana turned in bed for the third time in ten minutes. It was late afternoon on April 6, 1994. He wondered why he was back in the country when he could have been gone at this time. He thought about the vibrant streets of Kampala, where he used to be at this time of the year. He had an unease that was deeply rooted inside of him. He had tried going outside in the morning. Nothing had seemed out of the ordinary with his shop and his neighbors.

He had seen his business partner a few days earlier, and all he could think about was the opportunities that were waiting for him when he got back. His sister in the north had said his boys were doing well. He was almost thinking about telling his wife that he was bored here and wanted to be somewhere else. His business partner, an unmarried young man in his thirties, had informed him that with all the money he had, he could even open up an oil station. Gasana had never thought about oil stations before, but even if he was going to try it, he wasn't going to do it in Rwanda. Despite the fact that he was already well known in the business scene, he couldn't ignore the fact that his ethnicity was a problem.

He tossed again in bed, and the door to his room squeaked open. His wife slowly came in, avoiding awakening him. They'd been watching television when he yawned and retreated to the bedroom. His wife came in slowly and touched his arm.

"Honey, are you asleep?"

"No, I am not; what is it, dear?" He responded, his voice cacophonous. He coughed. "I can't seem to find sleep in me. I don't know why I feel restless."

"Honey, you're always restless when you're not working. Don't act like you don't normally hate being on vacation of any sort." His wife joked and softly touched his now-ruined afro. "I don't know why you insist on having this much hair, and I don't know how you find time in your busy schedule to do the hair."

"Darling, this hair is a part of my brand as a businessman. You see, I don't only want to be the richest man; I also want to be the most handsome, so those young boys that take care of themselves will not take you away from me! You look like how you did all those years ago when I was sneaking behind your parents house; therefore, I must remain the vigilant, charming, and youthful boy I was back then!" Gasana joked, getting up and wrapping her in his arms.

Enticed by his wife's beauty, boredom flew out of the window. As they continued to flirt, they ended up making love as the loving couple that they were. After that, they lay in bed tangled.

"Do you think we should invest in an oil station?" Gasana started.

"Who gave you the idea?" His wife asked.

"Jeffrey. He brought almost five million last Sunday." Gasana replied.

A little silence.

"Wait, you didn't tell me?"

"Yeah, I was waiting for the right time to tell you." Gasana said.

"It's always the right time to tell me things. You're indeed *my* richest and most handsome man."

"Yes, I fully agree. I agreed many, many years ago, and I agree for the rest of the years we have ahead, which will be many, many years ahead." Gasana cooed, kissing his wife's forehead.

"That's quite a serious promise."

"Yes, I am a man of my word; you know that better than anyone else in this world."

"Maybe after my mother. That woman made you sweat the most! Remember when she asked, how many cattles you have?" His wife chuckled, and Gasana sighed fondly.

"Don't even start!" Gasana said, laughter still in his voice, "She asked me even worse questions privately when you and your father weren't there. I know who you take after Darling, and in fact, we need to visit her. Sometime soon. I miss her fond stare whenever we visit her with our kids. It makes me feel like the luckiest man alive. She is so fierce and tender at the same time; it's very weird."

"I know, right. Our father, as you know him, is the pacifier of the house, but for some reason, we also went to our mother whenever we messed up big time. Like when you impregnated me." His wife said shyly.

"Well, what can I say? I feel like when she saw me, she understood why you fell for me. I mean, she must have been like, my daughter couldn't pull a better man. It's that she pulled him in just the wrong way, but he's worth it." They both laughed at his self-praising speech.

"Stop it! Anyway, regarding the oil station, you are already known among the good businessmen around. I think if you don't feel like you're going to be overwhelmed by the whole ordeal, you can do it. I support you always. It's just that I don't know how lucrative it is, how many people are agreeable to work with. There's no way I am going to quit my work at the ministry." Mama Anne said.

"I know, and I can't ask you to quit your job. However, I think I am scared." Gasana said, all the lightheartedness of earlier was gone. His wife gave his hand an assuasive squeeze; the one that usually made everything seem possible for him. Just not this time. He was too scared this time around. He was an intuitive man, and being a businessman had made him trust his instinct even more.

"You're usually never scared. I think the tension that has been around is fading off. We haven't heard much threatening news; it's back to that hate speech of theirs and weird publications all over. We're used to those, darling. Just ignore it and do your thing. You're good at this." Mama Anne reassured him.

"It's really not about my abilities as a businessman. It's about my ethnicity. Don't you think I would be in danger if I entered the oil station market too? That makes me even more of a threat. That way, I'll not only be a snake and an intruder but also a competition to them, one that has been accumulating wealth over the years. I consider myself lucky that I am alive with my family. Others have been caught, their houses have been ransacked, and tortured and..."

His wife kissed him, silencing his rant.

"Baby, can we go grab a beer in the bar somewhere? I suddenly want to go dancing." She suggested, and it worked.

"Just a bar? Not a hotel? Why do you always do this to me? I miss going out with you, actually. So, can you make yourself pretty, and we shall go?" Gasana said with a chuckle as his wife disappeared into the bathroom adjacent to their bedroom, and he joined her.

In an hour, they were ready to go.

"That dress looks very good, but it is also very old. Why didn't you put on the new one that I brought you last month?" Gasana complained as his wife made finishes to her simple make up of white Johnson powder, an eyebrow to her smoothly shaved eyebrows, and a lip gloss.

"We're just going to the bar in the village in the neighborhood; there is no need for that fancy dress. Besides, this one is a bit more freeing." Mama Anne said and headed out in front of her husband, who followed her out.

When they got outside, Donatha was sitting outside with Anne as they were preparing the beans to cook.

"Don't tell me you are planning to actually cook those beans tonight!" Mama Anne exclaimed.

"No, we just had the time, and we decided to do this. There is just enough to eat tonight." Donatha replied.

"I am glad she now knows how to actually remove the stones from the beans. Good job, Anne!" Gasana said.

"She's eight, not two! She even cleans her room and does other chores." Mama Anne chided her husband.

To Gasana, Anne was his little princess who needed to sit on her pretty crown, have her hair done well, her clothes ironed and perfumed, and have her food brought to her on silver platters and expensive china.

"Is that so? I will bring you something when I come home to applaud your good work. I didn't know that you had grown that much!" Gasana promised.

"Come on, it's nothing that serious; she's the only girl; she needs to learn this so that she will know how to manage her own household." Mama Anne averred.

"Mama, let Daddy bring me chocolate. After all, I haven't had any in some time." Anne chirped.

"Yes, I will, dear; your mother is just jealous." Gasana said and high-fived his daughter, who snickered at her mother.

"You know that I have work, right? I have my own money; I can buy my own chocolates!" Mama Anne said, "Dona, please get me my other sandals from inside."

At that moment, all Gasana could think about was how much he adored his family. Sometimes he wondered how he could videotape all those moments and watch them when he was away on business. It wasn't that important since they were engraved on the walls of his heart.

Unfortunately for the couple, the bar they were planning to go to was closed—the one that looked a bit posh in their area. They had no choice but to go to the one where Gasana had met Lando, Kalisa, and Matthieu. At the door of the shabby bar, they both peeked in to see a lot of people in the bar. It looked a bit weird to have that many clients on a Wednesday evening.

"There's surprisingly a lot of people here. Did you think we could find all these people?" Mama Anne said, sounding excited.

Gasana, on the other hand, wasn't feeling the same. The memories of meeting the other men, thrilled, only to be soaked in beer at the end of the night filled his brain. He tried to mask his disappointment because his wife looked exhilarated to be in the room, odorized by the mixture of perfumes and scents as well as the different beverages and grilled meats in the room. It almost looked as if people were having a party in the small bar.

The woman whom Gasana had seen flirting with the men was bending over a table full of men; they also looked like they had just come in. His eyes scanned the room until they landed on one of the men, Matthieu.

Matthieu got up and headed in their direction. He was still the same afro-haired, agreeable self. He greeted Gasana and his wife with glee, as if they were what he was missing to really start to enjoy his time.

"Matthieu, how have you been?" Gasana spoke loud enough to be audible over the small speakers that looked quite new. Perhaps the incident when they had poured beer on him had awakened the senses of the bar owners, so they had decided to finally get real speakers for music with the cassettes.

"I have been well for sure! Business has been going well. I see you're here with your beautiful wife, whom we don't see very often! May the love between you two keep prospering." Matthieu said, greeting Gasana's wife and offering her a very big grin from his smoke-stained teeth.

"We are well, and thank you for the well wishes." Mama Anne said shyly under the scrutiny of the man.

"Yeah, so did you come alone or are you here with friends and other men?" Gasana inquired. A flash of recognition appeared in Matthieu's eyes. They both knew what that meant. Even though he hadn't participated in the act of humiliating him, he had been an onlooker. Gasana had been pleasantly surprised that the news hadn't spread like wildfire all over the village as all other shameful incidents had.

"Oh, I came alone, but there is a family of another wealthy man who also just moved around here, just in the other house that your other friend used to occupy. It's astonishing how you two haven't met yet." Matthieu explained.

"I didn't know that the house was already occupied. Usually I am resting before I go back to work. You know how these things are, so I haven't had time to meet. I'll make sure to greet them on our way out. Now let me get my wife a place to sit and something to drink; we'll catch up later." Gasana said, conclusively, that she did not want to engage in more conversations with the man.

"Why would you sit alone when there is in fact an empty seat on our table? I think we can ask the lady to bring one more chair for you." Matthieu said. Though he was wary, Gasana didn't want anyone to notice.

"Sure, no problem. Hey, lady, can you bring one more chair to his table? Thank you." Gasana asked.

As Matthieu led them to the table, Gasana realized that his wife was starting to get bored with the whole experience that they were having.

"Don't worry, we're soon getting to the best part of the evening. I bet it's too early for serious music. Now they're just playing Congolese music; once they start dancing to the Rwandan ones, we'll stand up and attempt to dance. It just doesn't look like there is enough space to do so unless one were to remove these tables." He told his wife.

"Yes, you are right. Well, it looks like these are good people, let's at least get acquainted with them." Mama Anne said. Among other things that Gasana liked about his lady was that she wasn't the type to force things. She was always grateful for what she got from the moment.

If 'live and enjoy' the moment was a person, it'd be her.

Matthieu took them to the table, and he introduced them to the family of Innocent. The husband was called Innocent and the wife was called Martha, and they were business people as well; they owned farms in the countryside and sold the animals they reared for meat. Gasana was always happy to meet fellow business-oriented people. Despite the fact that he always went with his wife to the parties organized by the people inside the ministry where she worked,. He didn't enjoy it. He found them rigid and uncurious. They seemed to have the idea that life started and ended with government work. They weren't always ready to expand their thinking, as businesspeople were.

He also learned that the man, Innocent, was an influential Hutu extremist himself. He wasn't spoken about, but Matthieu had told him when his wife was conversing with their new neighbors that where he lived, he used to rattle on the Tutsis in the area for torture and robbery. This didn't sit well with Gasana.

However, they also conversed and found out that they shared a love for country life; they liked the same football teams; and when the business talk started, Innocent also mentioned that he was intrigued by the oil station businesses. This made them have an almost instantaneous connection as they talked about the pros and cons of the business. For a split moment, Gasana thought he had made a new acquaintance that would be with him for a very long period of time. It sounded like they could both benefit from each other's business experiences. Innocent also mentioned that he had taken his children, two sets of twins, to Kenya to be schooled there, and they were now living like newlyweds with his wife.

Gasana thought that this man could be a worth-it connection in an all-around sense, until he rethought about the fact that he was a Hutu man with a lot of money and a history of hating on Tutsi, which was who he was.

"I will be outside, smoking; let me know when you are planning to go home." Matthieu whispered to Gasana around eight thirty in the night. Gasana checked his own watch in the dimly lit bar and decided that they had had a good evening of fun and that they could go home.

"So, I think for us, we will just go home; it is actually late." Gasana announced to the table.

"Yes, you're right, Gasa, it's late; we've been here since the afternoon as well; Madam is tired; I have to get her home for a good and well-deserved sleep." Innocent responded. Among other things that Gasana liked about the man was that he was equally respectful and adoring of his wife as he was of himself. They shared a lot in common, minus their ethnicities.

"Alright, we are even neighbors; Mama Anne says you did not bring the car because it is near; we brought ours; do you mind if we give you a ride?" Martha said, smiling at the other woman fondly. It seemed that not only the men had had fun, but the women had bonded over some things as well. Gasana loved that for them.

"Alright, let's go." Innocent said that and put the cash on the table. "I am paying for us. I really liked meeting you! You're a man of business. We will be meeting some other time; you will buy then." Innocent was a big, burly man with a bald head. He took space, and he knew it. Next to him, Gasana's lean frame was almost half the man's size.

He had parked his Toyota around the edge of the shabby bar. As they were walking out, it looked like there was a commotion. The environment seemed restless, with people walking back and forth. When Gasana checked his watch, it was around 9. They all got into the Toyota, and Gasana and his wife sat at the back. Since they were not using the main road, Innocent drove them straight to their house, where they all said bye and got inside the house quickly. However, on the road, it looked like people were stopping other people from going on foot for a few minutes.

Gasana and his wife entered their home, checked on their child, and went straight to bed. Early in the morning, there was a knock on their door. It wasn't Anne's soft knock on the door telling them that it was time for breakfast; it wasn't a maid's knock that came to ask if they could give money to buy some groceries. It was a frantic knock that threatened to tear down the door if it didn't open as soon as possible.

"Who's there? I am coming." Gasana said as he got up and his wife tossed in bed. The clock hung next to their humongous wedding photo frame read 6 am in the morning.

"It's me, Donatha, please open!" Donatha cried.

"What happened?" Gasana asked as he opened the door to his room to see Donatha holding Anne's trembling hand.

"Papa Anne, something happened. You need to listen to the radio. The other maid, Kankindi and Zamu, are outside shouting for us to get outside so that they can kill us." Donatha said, trying her level best to speak calmly.

"Wait for a moment. Anne, come here." Gasana said, panic kicking in his system. "Make sure you close well. I will be out in a minute."

He took his trembling child inside, put on his clothes quickly, and woke his wife as quickly as possible as well.

"Anne, speak to me; everything will be well, dear, okay?" Gasana babbled. He didn't even know what to really say to his child now. He quickly switched on the radio on the nightstand.

Le Ministre de la défense a la profonde douleur d'annoncer au peuple rwandais la triste nouvelle du décès du chef de l'Etat, Son Excellence le général major Juvénal Habyarimana, suite à un accident d'avion survenu près de l'aéroport le 6 avril 1994 aux environs de 20 heures et demie, l'avion qui le ramenait de Dar es-Salaam ayant été descendu par des éléments ennemis non encore identifiés...

The Minister of Defense is deeply saddened to announce to the Rwandan people the sad news of the death of the Head of State, His Excellency Major General Juvénal Habyarimana, following a plane crash near the airport on April 6, 1994, around 8:30 p.m., the plane bringing him back from Dar es Salaam having been shot down by as yet unidentified enemy elements.

Gasana turned off the radio and sat down next to his wife, who was also listening to the radio, as well as their daughter.

"This is very, very bad news." Mama Anne whispered under her breath.

"I know."

Gasana looked out the window and saw his houseguard standing on top of his expensive car. He knew that this was the time when things were going south.

Gasana told his wife to stay inside the house while he went outside to check on the situation. Donatha was looking at Zamu and Kankindi, who were standing outside and starting to shout that they had taken enough from 'inyenzi' cockroaches; enough was enough, and they were going to take their rightful place.

Gasana decided to face death in the eye and opened the door. "Zamu, what is going on?" when

"It's over; enough is enough. You have killed our father; now you pay for it! I have worked as hard as possible. I have called on the people that will help me finish you." Zamu said.

"I don't know what you're talking about. I have never treated you differently. I have always paid you on time. What do you mean that enough is enough?" Gasana asked, willing himself to not tremble under the hateful eye of his houseguard, who was sporting a shiny machete.

"It's your arrogance that I don't like. You have been a boss for me; however, now all you own is mine. This is the moment that I have been waiting for." Zamu said and squatted on top of the car.

"Alright, let's not talk as boss and employee now; can't we talk as a man to a man?" Gasana proposed. At this point, he knew that things were not easy. He could hear voices of people marching and people crying. From the top of the hill where his house was, he could see smoke as well. It was only his house that had this amount of peace. Though he couldn't say it was any peace at all.

Zamu's evil laugh at his proposal told him that he wasn't going to listen to any bargains.

"The last time a snake bargained and talked to a human being, humanity ended in trouble. I will have no discussion with you. However, since you have been my boss for so long, I will let you choose how I kill you. However, Donatha must be mine. She will have to be mine. She will give me whatever I want from her today. Bring her now!"

"Calm down, come in, and let's talk." Gasana pleaded with the man. Zamu considered his employer for a second and hooped down from the car.

"Alright, how much?"

"Thirty thousand."

"Are you out of your mind?"

"Fifty."

"That buys you a day, but doesn't guarantee that you will live tomorrow." Zamu retorted, "The boys should be somewhere near here now."

Right then, a troop of young men that used to carry things to the shops entered, all wielding different types of armor, machetes, grenades on their belts, guns, and hatchets.

At the sight of it. Gasana felt a tear fall down his cheek. His money, his businesses, and all his possessions almost meant nothing. He wasn't a coward, but still, he couldn't fight off fifteen young men who were armed.

"I will give you three hundred thousand, but just let me and my family go!" Gasana shouted out of desperation.

"How about we go in and look for that money and other cockroaches that you're hiding in there?" one of the young men said.

"No, stop; it's okay; I will handle this. Everyone will get their cut, as we agreed. Remember, it's me who brought you here." Zamu said. Despite the unity of their evil to kill and exterminate the Tutsi, it seemed that when it came to looting, everyone wanted what they could for themselves.

"Alright, if you agree, tell them to go away; you and I can sort this out, and you will divide the money amongst yourselves." Gasana told Zamu, who had been interested, the moment three hundred was mentioned.

After that, Zamu talked to the men, and they left. Gasana gave him the money, and later on, he locked himself in his room, where his wife and child sat, sad and hopeless.

His usually bubbly and fierce wife seemed like she had been doused with ice-cold water, there was no more fire in her eyes. She looked defeated.

"What about our boys?" She asked. "Can you be able to call?"

"Do you think we're able to call at this moment?" Gasana snapped. He knew that he shouldn't. "I am sorry, dear. I don't think so."

"What do we do?"

"I am not sure."

"Are we going to die, mama?" Anne's bleak voice cut through their backs and forth.

"No, darling, we are going to be fine. God will keep us safe. If anything goes wrong, run. Run as fast as you can." Mama Anne said.

"Anne, you won't have to run. Papa is always here for you. Now that the bad men are gone, go get breakfast and be in your room reading books after that. Okay?" Gasana soothed her.

When Anne was gone, Gasana held his wife's hands and looked into her eyes.

"I love you so much, as do my children. I am not sure what to do right now, but if I die, I will die with you."

"I know, and I love you too. However, we need to do something. Can't you call a friend or something? Can't we go find our children up there? Can't we find someone to leave Anne with?" She asked.

Gasana sighed and shook his head. He had connections and friends, but he wasn't sure anyone could help. They could try fleeing like everyone else was doing; otherwise, if they stayed, sooner or later, they would be killed.

An hour later, Gasana wondered why there hadn't been any more troops of men coming to look for them. He thought Zamu had wanted to monopolize the loot at his house, and he was right.

The whole day went off without a hitch. It almost looked like a normal day except that the only music played was of killing Tutsis, the only news was information of where they were hiding, the only sounds were screams, cries, orders, and gunshots, and the only character was death.

During the night, around when it was dark, the troop came back again. This time, they did not want to discuss; they wanted money, food, furniture, and blood.

Gasana and his family, along with Donatha, were told to kneel on their carpet in the living room. The five men towered above them with machetes and guns. Then Zamu came in.

"This is a good time to take what is ours. Kankindi, I want you to look in the house and find the money, the jewelry, and everything valuable. Donatha, get ready, you and I will have fun in the master bedroom today, we need to feel what the wealthy snakes felt on that expensive bed." He said, pacing the living room.

"As for him, hit his feet so that he can feel how we feel when we walk while he sits in that expensive car of his!" Zamu ordered, and they started hitting Gasana's feet and legs. "In fact, his wife too!" They also took on Mama Anne's legs.

After an hour of beating their legs, even the men were tired of waiting for the boss's order. They quarreled about whether Zamu was just using them to get revenge on his employers or not. They decided to ask Zamu if he was planning to kill them or if they should do it themselves and continue looting.

"Okay, let's give them a moment for their last words, and we will finish them and move on. Except for Donatha, she's mine." Zamu concluded.

"Please, for the sake of the times that I helped you and all the years we lived together, let me and my family leave here tonight. I promise you that we will find somewhere to go if you let us leave alive!" Gasana pleaded.

"You will kill me, but I will not let you do whatever you want with me." Donatha said, seething with anger.

"Why are you doing this? It's not like I will resurrect; you can only kill me once!" Mama Anne shouted at the killers.

Chapter 3

As Mama Anne shouted, Zamu and his men laughed out loud and villainously. However, a flash of realization hit them. They were bloodthirsty; however, they'd get her blood only once. It was as if they wanted to kill them, resurrect them, and kill them all over again.

However, as they kept beating Gasana in the sores of his feet with his wife and child there watching along with their housemaid, Donatha, a voice took the whole crowd off guard. Innocent's burly frame filled the door to the porch, and everyone's attention was switched to him. Regaining their composure, the troop pointed their weapons at him. However, Zamu, who was leading the entire team, seemed to bow out a little bit.

"Hello, sir, guys, put those weapons down; this is one of ours," he ordered.

"I thought you knew that I live next door; my wife is asleep. Why couldn't you do this killing business during the day? Must you bother me? Do you know who I am?" Innocent asked, his voice commanding and sour.

Gasana started to wonder whether he was the same man they had just shared drinks with the previous day. Perhaps Matthieu had been right; Innocent seemed pretty influential. If the troops recognized him, then he must have some level of respect among them. Gasana's feet were sore with pain—pain that seemed to numb every other part of his body. He felt even dizzy because of the beating in the sores of his feet. However, nothing was as painful as watching his family, whom he was supposed to be protecting, tremble with fear.

"Take this money and a few things that you have already collected and leave; I don't want to hear from you again. I don't want to see you here again either; these are my predators from now on." Innocent commanded, "Wait, I need two of you to help me escort the husband and wife to my house. Quickly. I will take care of them from there. Leave the maid and the child alone; when it is their time, I will come back for them."

Zamu and one of his men tied up Gasana and Mama Anne and escorted them to Innocent's house. It wasn't too far, but as a businessman, he didn't have to make his hands touch any blood while there were enough pawns in his vicinity to do the dirty work.

As they got Gasana and his wife to Innocent's house, he ordered the killers to lock them in a guest room. He didn't bother repeating himself; Zamu and his one other troop fellow left immediately after he tossed them a bundle of two thousand notes. It was evident that Innocent might have been a feared man; even the killers were afraid of him.

He looked at the wife and husband, smiled knowingly, and left them there. Inside, Gasana and Mama Anne heard him lock the door and remove the key. As soon as they heard his footsteps fade out, Mama Anne broke down into tears, but she held a hand on her mouth.

Gasana pulled her into his chest, and he cried silently as well. He had never felt helpless in his entire life. He was wondering how he had gotten here. He prided himself on being the pillar of his family, but now that he was being shaken, everyone around him would no doubt waver. His wife, a proud woman whom he had forgotten had any tears in her, was now crying and sobbing in his chest.

He had failed his family, but he had to be steadfast; he had to come up with the most convincing proposal for Innocent. From the discussions he had had with the man, he could tell that he was not just hate-driven; he was a money-driven person. He swayed with profit. Wave it in his face, and he would listen. Gasana could see that Innocent was interested in accumulating generational wealth. He would do anything that would make him richer in ten years to come rather than a present income that he would spend in a week. He already had money to spend; now he wanted to loot for three more generations. Gasana understood him. He was a businessman himself.

The more he thought about his businesses and his money, the more he felt helpless. He was unable to use the money he had. He felt like he had wasted his time looking for all that money. He wondered what he was going to do. Listening to his wife's cries broke his heart into thousands of pieces, and to think that none of them had done anything, their only crime was that they were human beings who had no influence on where they were born or which ethnic group they were from.

As a literate man, he knew that this wasn't society's fault; it was all propaganda. This was bad governance. The tension had built up over the years; their ethnicity had been tortured for decades; it was just the last straw. The bad politicians were now using the citizens to kill other citizens. He knew that if one had been mentally fed that their neighbors were snakes and cockroaches at home, then at school, then at work, they'd at some point want to get rid of them.

He knew this wasn't the right time to use his intellect; however, going into the philosophy of the situation was keeping him busy in his brain. He was trying to shift the blame from anyone; there was a political mastermind behind the killings. He tried to be stoic about the entire thing.

"Why did this happen to us? What crime did we commit?" His wife croaked out.

"I really don't know." Gasana said it noncommittally.

"What is going to happen to our children?" Mama Anne asked.

"I really don't know," Gasana repeated.

"Can you say something else? Something nice? Tell me we're not going to die; tell me everything will be fine." Mama Anne pleaded in between sobs.

"I can't, honey. I am as helpless as you are in this situation. I am only thinking that the best thing we can do is to go to sleep first. The only thing we can do is trust in God for survival." Gasana reasoned with her. He knew that it's impossible to attain sleep.

"You might as well like me to fly as well." Mama Anne said, dryly.

"Let's not argue, dear wife; I have trust that we are going to get through this, by God's grace." Gasana said. He was now starting to realize that God was their last resort. There was nothing they could do; there was no one they could trust. Only God could spare their lives at this moment.

They both went quiet after that. Gasana held his wife silently and tucked her into the fluffy, well-made bed. Gasana couldn't stop pacing around the room restlessly. He couldn't sleep, knowing fully well that three of his children were out there, in between life and death. He tried the window, but it wasn't possible to pass through. The metallic rods weren't to be trifled with. Finally, he decided to join his wife in bed.

The morning came, but it arrived later than the rest of the mornings, when the birds chirped outside. Gasana woke up. He could negotiate with Innocent, man to man. They could make pacts; he'd rather be anywhere than locked in here, wondering how his offspring had survived or not.

His wife, who was usually a heavy sleeper, was also awake the moment she felt him turn in bed. They both woke up.

"Good morning, let's try to knock on the door; let them come to open so that we can negotiate."

Mama Anne suggested and went on to do that without Gasana, who closed his eyes, pushing back the tears that had formed in his eyes. He had worked so hard in his life to avoid helplessness, but now he decided that fate was fate. His wife's knocks on the door intensified by a minute. After twenty minutes of knocking without an answer, she leaned against the door and sobbed quietly.

Gasana pushed his tall frame out of bed and hugged his wife tightly for a long minute before they were startled by a key turning in the lock.

Abruptly, Martha, Innocent's wife, entered, carrying a tray of two tea cups, slices of bread, and an omelet.

"Good morning. Please eat quietly, as fast as you can, before he wakes up. If he knew that I fed you, he might get us all killed." She whispered.

"I don't want to eat anything when I am not sure if my children are even alive, let alone well fed." Mama Anne said bitterly.

"You have to eat, darling; how will we be able to move along if we haven't eaten? Martha is being as nice and welcoming as she can; please don't let her efforts go in vain." Gasana reasoned.

"Alright, I will leave when you're done; there is no time; if he found any evidence that I fed you, he'd kill me with his bare hands." Martha whispered again.

Gasana got the impression that this was more than just their situation; perhaps their marriage was rooted in fear. Maybe the happy sight the other day in the bar was a charade. This woman seemed terrified of her husband. It was evident that the wife had been traumatized by Innocent's monstrous ways.

"Thank you very much." They ate the bread and eggs, taking big gulps of the milk tea. In a few minutes, they were done.

"Can you please let us out? We'll be very quiet. I just need to go check on my daughter, please." Mama Anne pleaded, but Martha refused.

"If he doesn't find you here where he left you, he'd come, find you, and kill you immediately, and he wouldn't spare me either. Please just stay here. This is the best I can do." Martha said, left the room, and locked them again.

"She makes sense; the best option we have now is to bargain with him." Gasana proposed. "That was a much-needed breakfast; let's hope he comes back."

To their misery, Innocent did not open the door until 3 in the afternoon. He was carrying a tray with meat.

"I have some food for you; this is some of my dog's leftovers. I gather you'd even eat those since you haven't eaten since yesterday. Rich people like you must be new to hunger." Innocent said as he situated himself in a chair next to the wardrobe.

"I at least kept you in a warm place; other snakes are now back where they belong, out in the bushes. I am such a kind man." Innocent boasted. He was probably also more twisted in the head than Gasana had anticipated.

"Yes, you are. Thank you for the hospitality and warm welcome. However, I'd like to talk to you; we're not too hungry." Gasana said. He was now feeling trepidation on his forehead.

"Um, even your wife; she's not hungry; I like them strong; maybe you'll let me taste how lucky you have been over the years." Innocent said. Gasana clenched his teeth but said nothing to that, as he didn't want anger and jealousy to get the best of him.

"Well, I wanted to talk to you about money." Gasana started. "I have businesses all around East Africa; I will give you some of them; you'll give me protection and freedom for my family in return."

Innocent burst out laughing.

"Are you really saying that? I could kill you all and get all you possess; I don't need you to give them to me; after all, everything you own was meant to be ours. You are just the extras in the country." Innocent retaliated.

"Well, maybe you can capture everything I own here in Rwanda, but in other countries, you'll need my lawyers; you'll need a letter between you and me to possess it." Gasana refuted.

Innocent sighed deeply and decided that the man was knowledgeable about what he was doing.

"I will cut to the chase; I speak with money and profits only, as you already know. I will only allow your wife to go where you keep the papers; bring them to me; you'll sign to me your businesses; and I will let you go." He gave them a nefarious look and left the room.

"Gasana, you remain here; only your wife goes. I have claimed you; no one will kill you. I only have the power to kill you. Now, hurry up before I change my mind." Innocent said.

Mama Anne got up and ran towards their house. Her mind was set on finding the papers and hoping to see that her child was still safe and untouched. One could not just rely on the word of a murderer. Innocent had mentioned that no one would kill them, but they couldn't be so sure. He was evil.

Upon arriving home, Donatha was seated in the destroyed living room with Anne, who ran to her mother in tears.

"Ma, where were you the entire night? I couldn't see you at all. I thought you had left me alone." Anne cried.

"Mama would never do such a thing. I am with you; please be calm, okay? Be a good girl who doesn't cry. I am coming to pick up some things, but I will be back tonight to pick you up. I have a very short time." Mama Anne promised.

She looked at Donatha, who looked even worse.

"Has she eaten yet?" She asked her housemaid.

"Yes, she has, but just a bit; she has refused to eat enough food. The other troop did not come back, but Zamu came back to threaten me. I am not sure how long we are going to be safe here." Donatha vented.

"Don't worry, we're negotiating with Innocent; God willing, we'll be able to finally be able to flee with his help. Be ready; anytime, we might come back to pick you two up." Mama Anne instructed. Donatha nodded her head rigorously and watched her employer rush to the masterbed, which was also a bit of a wreck as the previous troop of killers had made everything chaotic.

Mama Anne went into the room and removed the mat slightly under the bed to expose a small safe that had been built into the house to fetch the papers and a stack of cash. She rushed back to the living room and gave Donatha the stack of cash.

"Please hide the money from you; find somewhere to put the money. Just in case anything happens. God only knows. Please stay safe with my daughter until we come back to take you with us." Mama Anne said, gave her daughter a hurried hug, and ran back to Innocent's house.

Upon arriving there, she found Innocent and his wife, Margret, arguing in the living room. She hid outside to eavesdrop before entering.

"They're Tutsis, and they must die. That's final!" Innocent roared.

"What do you mean they must die? You promised them to let them go as long as they signed you that you're the heir to their things. I know they might not even survive, but just don't let their blood be on your hands. Just help them this once." Martha pleaded.

"You know I hate to repeat myself, so don't let me repeat that I have nothing to do with snakes! I must help the government and everyone to free the country of the excess animals that have invaded our country since long ago. This is our chance! If you don't agree, I can get you killed with them." Innocent retorted.

Mama Anne realized that the man had never had any intentions of letting them go or anything. She tore one of the papers she had brought and disposed of the pieces before entering. Innocent smiled like the monster he was at the sight of her.

"Very well, right now, we can proceed with the agreement."

They proceeded with signing the papers and giving him more paperwork that contained the specifics of different registered businesses. However, when they were done, Innocent refused to let them go; instead, he locked them up in the guest room with the sinewy dog meat plate.

Gasana and Mama Anne paced around the room, wondering what they were going to do after giving away the businesses, hoping that the man would help them.

"He wasn't planning on helping us or letting us go." Gasana mused.

"No, he wasn't. I overheard them talking. He doesn't just want money; he wants our blood." Mama Anne said, on the verge of tears, but she refused to let them fall. This wasn't the time to cry. It was time to accept their death and embrace it with open arms.

Silently, they waited for any sign of a person to come back with good news, but nobody came until the night fell. They'd heard cries and shootings, and each time they heard those, they couldn't stop wondering whether it was one of their children, their neighbor, or their family who was crying or dying.

After some time, when they had lost hope, they heard a key open the door again. It was Martha.

"Come with me. He has finally agreed to let you go. The only problem is that he hasn't agreed to protect you. We'll let you go back to your house now, try to get money, and drive your car away." She explained.

This was more like, There's a hungry lion at the door, but I will just let you go.

"But that was not our agreement; he said he'd help us escape!" Mama Anne cried.

"I know he did; he's a monster. Thank God he even listened to me and agreed to let you go." Martha said. "Now, hurry up before he changes his mind."

Gasana knew he had to take responsibility and guard his family. He had bargained for freedom and security, but he was only given freedom. He couldn't be a fool. He knew the man could have killed them with his bare hands and fed them to his dog, but he didn't. They'd find a way.

They got up quickly, thanked Martha, and went to their house. Upon arriving, it was very dark, and Gasana searched for a torch and lit their chaotic living room. It looked like the windows had been broken, more things had been taken from the house than what they had left, and worst of all, Donatha and Anne were nowhere to be found.

"Where could she have taken my child?" Mama Anne cried.

"I don't know!" Gasana shouted.

"No, they can't have killed my child!" She cried even more.

They searched their house as carefully as they could, careful not to call too loud and wake up the sleeping killers in the neighborhood, but there was no response. When they found no one, Gasana decided to drag his wife to their car to check if it was at least going to help them, but it wasn't working.

***

Donatha kept walking down a small dirt road that would lead her into the bushes near the swamp, with Anne on her back. She couldn't say she wasn't tired, but there was no better time to move than now. Cricket and frog sounds around her were so eerie, but she kept going.

She had decided that she wasn't going to allow herself to be raped by Zamu, and she wasn't going to let them kill Anne without trying her best to save the child. As she kept walking, the horrific events of the past two days were all catching up with her.

Zamu came to their house, bringing in a troop, and they invaded their house, threatening to kill and rape her.

The pungent smell of dead bodies and blood in the bushes was also very strong. She encountered more than three bodies as she went; in her entire life, she had never seen a dead person at all. Now, it seemed, the country was all full of bodies.

When she got tired as they reached the bushes near the swamp, she decided to put Anne down and rest. She couldn't tell what time it was, but it was dead at night. She wondered whether she would make it to the Nyabugogo River or not. Either way, she needed a break. Her back and neck were sore from carrying an eight-year-old, but it wasn't time to complain. She had packed some of the food and clothes in a bag that she carried.

She gave Anne a banana and peeled hers as well.

"Dona, where are we going?" Anne asked.

"I don't know either," Donatha replied.

"Where are my parents? Are they going to come find us?" Anne asked again, tears threatening to fall.

"I really don't know. There were bad people trying to kill us, and I decided to take you away from them. I don't know much of anything else, Anne." Donatha responded. Her heart was shattered for a young girl whose childhood was going to be forever stained with this history, if they would survive.

Donatha had decided that since she knew where her grandparents lived, they'd flee there. They continued eating the bananas, but it wasn't long until Anne started to cry for her mother.

"Dona, please show me my mother, please!"

"Anne, I don't know; there was nothing I could do." Donatha replied, but it didn't help as Anne's cries heightened by a minute.

"Ma, Mamaa," Anne cried.

Donatha decided that if they remained there, someone would hear them, and that would be one of their worst nights.

"Anne, I will tell you something. Let's walk again; we're going to see your grandma. Don't you miss her? Your mother will find you there, alright?" The child nodded, and her sobs reduced as they kept walking.

They couldn't see exactly where they were going, but Donatha held Anne's hand, and they walked through the thick bushes as fast as they could. By early morning, they'd reached the river Nyabarongo, and so had Interahamwe, waiting for their victims.

Chapter 4

Upon reaching the banks of the Nyabarongo River in Nyabugogo, Donatha held Anne's hand and a bag of the essentials that she should have needed in the other arm. They hid behind the bushes as they watched the guerillas stop people at a barrier. One woman went ahead and showed her identity, but then there was something that looked like an argument. In a blink of an eye, they pulled her aside and chopped her head off. Donatha gasped but quickly covered the child's eyes. She realized that this was useless. Yes, Anne was a child, but in this one instance, she would witness more on their way to finding refuge. She had to get used to this. This was their reality at the time.

A couple more minutes passed, and Donatha deduced that she had to continue no matter what. If she could get to Nyabugogo, where the cars stopped, she'd be able to finally get on a bus or a lift towards Gitarama, where Anne's grandparents lived.

"Where are you going?" One of the Interahamwe asked Donatha when she wanted to try to cross the border.

"I'd like to go to Gitarama with my child here; it's insecure where we are." Donatha responded, hoping that they wouldn't just assume she was Tutsi.

"Hehe, it has to be insecure for a while as we do the clean-up of all the cockroaches." the young man responded, "Now, show me your ID; you're a beautiful woman with a beautiful child; if you're lucky, your ID will not be of a cockroach."

"I think you will have to really forgive me this time; my mother in the countryside has my ID; I don't have it with me. Will you let me pass?" Donatha said.

"I don't buy it, lady. Do you see that pile of people there? They had the same excuse. They're simply trying to save their worthless lives, but we are on a mission. We are cleaning up the country as good citizens should." The young man replied villainously, baring his teeth and bulging out his eyes to look as scary as he could.

"Please, why would I be too confident to show up here if I were a Tutsi, even with my child? I wouldn't do that. I really am not." Donatha said, but the man wasn't listening; he was already having his back at them, calling upon the men who had been pulling dead bodies out of the road to make space, pushing them into the thick bushes, and throwing others into Nyabarongo.

"Listen, listen, if you see another one trying to escape with the excuse of no ID card, just pull them aside and cut one limb at a time so that even in their next lives, they won't dare to lie." The man declared, and the rest of the interahamwe laughed and cheered on.

Anne looked at the bloody machetes raised, then back at Donatha, unsure whether to cry or to run away from these scary-looking men. Even in school, they hadn't learned about monsters that were as scary as these. All the horror stories she had read or listened to were not as scary as this moment right here. She wondered what had happened to her parents and her brothers. A tear escaped her eye, but she wiped it off and clutched Donatha's skirt tighter than before.

Miraculously, a young man appeared in the crowd with a brand new-looking machete, as if he had just joined right then. Donatha recognized him from the workers that used to frequent Gasana's shop in their neighborhood. His name was Nganji. He was cheered on and placed in front of the men, who congratulated him on his brave decision to contribute to the 'clean-up'.

"Nganji, Nganji!" Donatha called out.

"Shut up, young lady! We are keeping you and that baby of yours for a spectacular show. We will use you as an example of why no one should lie to us. We will chop your limbs one by one after we sample you! Right guys?" The scary-looking young man shouted.

"Nganji, Nganji!" Donatha shouted again.

"Nganji, this woman claims that she doesn't have her ID and that she is Hutu; is it true?" the man asked Nganji, who looked at the man square in the eye and responded. "Can I see her? I know a ton of women, you know."

"Here she is," the man said, pushing Donatha and Anne into the middle of the group of men who had blood-stained tools.

"Oh her, yes, I know her. I think she wasn't informed about leaving before; our parents in the countryside know each other well, so let me try to get her away from here; not having her ID can be very dangerous." Nganji responded, surprisingly sure of his own words. Donatha sighed with relief as the men calmed down and let Nganji take her with him.

When they were about 200 meters from the group, Donatha and Anne started to walk slower.

"Please hurry; if they know that you're not who you say you are, it can alert them. It would take them less than 30 seconds to kill us all." Nganji said.

"Thank you so much; I don't know how I will ever repay you. For someone who doesn't even know me that well, I just used to see you at the shop." Donatha said that and picked up the pace. "But why are you doing this?"

"It's my duty. I have to go with what my parents expect of me." Nganji responded non-comitally.

"But you don't have to do this, you know; you can just remain at home." Donatha said, but Nganji just chuckled and raised his machete to greet a group of men that bypassed them.

"We don't have choices. We are all meant to kill or inform the killers; otherwise, we also get killed for not killing. A friend of your enemy is also an enemy." He said. His burly, short frame looked so defeated from behind. He was usually a young man who would show up at the shop and flirt with the girls or shoot out pointless jokes, but his jolly nature was nowhere to be found. He was now supposed to take lives, not entertain them.

Donatha and Anne followed him in silence, feeling a little bit safe now that they had an ally. However, they worried that he might have just helped them lure them into a worse situation. They didn't have much to lose anyway. They'd have died like thirty minutes before if he hadn't appeared and said he knew them.

For some reason, Nganji seemed respected by the groups of interahamwe that passed. Donatha wondered what he had achieved or done.

"Can I ask you a question, though?" She queried

"Hmm,"

"Do you think we will be able to get a car to Gitarama from here?"

"I am not sure; we will try to find one; if we don't, I will have to just do what's possible. At the end of the day, I am also kind of risking myself here." He said.

When they reached a parked station, people were packed there, trying to enter the cars and escape the horrors.

"Wait here; I will speak with someone and come back for you." He said that and rushed towards a Toyota pickup that was parked a few meters from them.

"Is he going to get us a car that can take me to my mother?" Anne asked, but Donatha harrumphed, suppressing her laughter. She just wanted to laugh at the innocence of the small child after all they had been through. She was at a loss for words. She wondered whether she should rebuke her for being so childish or promise her that they would see her parents where they were going. However, no option would help. All Donatha was focused on was surviving, at least until they got to the countryside.

"I am not sure we will see your mother there. I just want to keep you safe, Anne; that's all that matters right now." Donatha said. This wasn't a time for little flowery lies that people fed to children. This was a scary moment that kept your blood pressure and adrenaline rush at their highest. It was a moment of ultimate despair where people who didn't have a crime had to die to satisfy the blood thirsty hounds of humans.

"Alright, here is what we are going to do. Donatha, take the child and go into the back of that car. There is my girlfriend, who is pregnant as well, and the driver is my cousin, so I think you two should be safe. He is rich and well known, and even though they will ask him to show people in his car, he will keep up with the story that you guys left your IDs with your parents. This is all I can do at this moment. I am sorry for everything." Nganji said as he escorted them to the white Toyota pickup.

Donatha felt tears stinging her eyes, but she didn't let them fall. She helped Anne into the backseat and got in as well.

"Thank you so much, Nganji. I will never forget this." She simply said, and the driver pulled up the windows.

"Good morning," Donatha greeted the pregnant lady in the back. She wore a dress made from kitenge with a hijab as well.

"Good morning," the lady mumbled back.

"My name is Donatha; I know Nganji from the shop of my employer, and this is Anne, a child of my employer." Donatha introduced herself.

"My name is Nadia." The pregnant lady said, evasively. It was as if she didn't want to have any conversation at all with them.

The car started moving, and the man in the car hadn't spoken a word to Donatha and Anne either. It seemed that every now and then, they'd be stopped, their car would be checked, the soldiers would look suspiciously in the backseat, and Donatha tried so hard not to look terrified. At some point they'd be stopped, and the man driving would end up having a long talk with the soldiers, which would cease once some money was slid into their hands.

Donatha hated the deafening silence in the car at first, but then she appreciated that she was able to doze off and have Anne sleep a bit more as they hadn't slept the previous night. There were sounds of bullets, cries, and screams as they went; sometimes they'd see bodies of people lying in the road, lifeless. Nadia looked at them through the window as she couldn't care less, and Donatha wondered if she wasn't escaping as well, but rather just moving. Her eyes were full of spite, and her constantly pursed lips made her look mean and hateful.

"Where are we? I will get off at *Mu Byimana* myself." Donatha asked when she realized that they were near their stop.

Through the interior rearview, the driver nodded at them, as if to say, "I remember."

As they entered the dirt roads near where she would get off, she wondered what she would do when she met Interahamwe on the road with a child. Would she keep lying until she got to Anne's grandparents'? Would she meet anyone from her family, or had they already fled? She had a lot of questions running through her mind that she didn't notice when the car stopped for them to get off until Anne tugged at her arm.

"This is where you get off, right?" The driver, who hadn't spoken a word to them for nearly three hours, said

"Oh, yes, this is it. Thank you very much, and please thank Nganji again when you see him." Donatha replied as she opened the door and took Anne off as well. Nadia mumbled a bye to them, and the car revved off the muddied road.

The streets were empty, unlike what she had anticipated on her way, but the pungent smell of dead bodies was strong; there were multiple marks on the land where bodies had been pulled.

"It smells so bad here." Anne remarked, echoing Donatha's thoughts.

"It's alright, dear; let's just go see your grandparents. You remember the route there,right?" Donatha asked Anne, who nodded her head vigorously in response, making the beads in her hair clink together. She felt a tad bit excited that, at least, she was going to see her grandparents.

Considering the voices of people from afar, Donatha decided that to avoid the risk of meeting the killers, passing through the small paths would be better. There would probably be a risk of plants with thorns, but that would be better than the sight of a machete or a club.

Donatha led the path through the bushes; she didn't even get time to marvel at the beauty of the diverse plans—aloe vera, mint, and useful grass—for this wasn't a time to be in awe; it was a time to cry for Mother Nature, whose body was now poisonous with victims' blood and bodies rooting deep in pits they had dug in different places.

After walking for half an hour, luckily they had not met anyone harmful, just other people hiding in bushes or walking to god-knows-where, for there was nowhere to go. They could see the baked brick house with clay tile roofing, with some smoke lingering around it. At first, Donatha thought that they had burned the house, but she realized that they could be cooking from the house. She wondered how they were so brave enough to cook in this condition.

"Ouch, I think there are some thorns in these bushes." Anne said as she looked at the small dot of blood on her finger where the thorn had pricked her.

"Watch out for those, walk carefully, and don't touch the plants, alright?" Donatha said. "We're almost there."

And they did reach there. Safe.

"Good afternoon!" Donatha called out, just enough for people indoors to hear, but no one responded.

She sent Donatha inside and went to check in the small kitchen. She then realized that the smoke had been coming from the stump of a eucalyptus tree that had been roughly split and put into the hearth. She removed it and sprinkled it with water. It looked as if they had been cooking and just ate as well.

"Yoo, Dona, it's you!" Anne's grandmother exclaimed when she came out and saw Donatha. "You're still alive, my child. I don't know how to thank God that you are here with my granddaughter. Mother Mary knew that I needed her here at least."

"Yes, grandma, it wasn't easy; we really survived by the grace of God; we had no hope either." Donatha said.

"You're brave. Ever since this disaster broke out, no one really knows what to do. The youthful people have just escaped to save their lives, but me and my old man here have no life left anyway. All we can do is simply wait for God's wishes. We will either survive or not, but we can't manage to run." Grandma replied. "Please get some potatoes there in the kitchen and eat. It must have been quite a long journey to get here."

Donatha nodded and went inside to fetch two plastic plates to serve food.

"I think there is some leftover milk inside a jug. Please get some for yourself and Anne." The old woman said, as she brought a bench for them to sit on while they ate.

"Grandma, I think it is better if we sit inside. It looks like it might rain." Donatha said.

"Yeah, you're right; it looks like it might. Let's go inside so you can greet the old man too. He is so down and afraid, but what can we do, my child? We will just keep praying to Jesus and Mother Mary for deliverance from this evil that has fallen on us." Grandma replied and led them inside with the bench.

Throughout the next couple of minutes, they caught up on what had happened together as the old man sipped his banana beer from his favorite gourd.

Donatha and Anne sat on the woven mat with their grandmother, while the old man sat on an armchair.

"I wonder where my child has wandered to. In such a big world, it's no longer big enough to hide us." Grandpa lamented.

"I would be lying if I said I knew where they are right now. As I was saying, we were betrayed by a house guard we had, but his plan was interrupted by some powerful man who took my boss and his wife. We only saw Madam one last time, but when the men came back to rape and kill us, I just decided that I would fight for my life and Anne's. It's been about a week or so since the boys left to go visit their aunt in Ruhengeri; we never got any more news about them at all." Donatha recounted.

"This war is going to finish our children off with spears and clubs; I wish we at least had a phone. I don't think there is a way to send these letters people send sometimes." Grandpa sighed.

"Ahaa, grandpa, it's all in God's hands. I am wondering how you haven't been killed yet, and you are here without even hiding." Donatha asked.

"My child, we don't have the strength to go hide in the churches, which is also useless," our neighbor said. Everyone who fled there was killed anyway. It was just a ruse to get everyone into the churches and kill them all at once with their grenades and rifles." Grandpa said, "We decided to stay here and bribe them with some of our cows and other domestic animals. Have you seen any chickens, rabbits, or most of our cows? We have been telling them to come pick them up whenever the husband of Mukabagorora comes home. They let us live in return. We don't know what will happen when we no longer have anything to give them. We don't even want to think about it now."

Donatha grieved the lives of these old people, who had probably been hoping to see their great-grandchildren. They were healthy, but then again, not healthy enough to survive this nightmare.

"Mukabagorora never helped you? I thought he was a good neighbor of yours." Donatha said.

"Ahaa, my child, didn't they invite us with a lot of other people in this neighborhood for the baptism of their new baby? Wasn't Vincent from across the mountain the godfather and his wife the godmother? But rumor has it that it's Mukabagorora's husband who killed them both. They set their house and barns on fire while all the windows and doors were closed. They died there, along with all of their children. It's no longer about who knows who; these people have turned into monsters. Who knew that he would kill people whom he used to like and invite?" Grandma expressed.

"I was planning to go greet Mukabagorora; I guess I shouldn't." Donatha said as her stomach churned. They had fled, but the neighbor of their temporary shelter was the renowned killer in their neighborhood.

The conversation about all of the sinister things happening made Anne's stomach churn with fear. She was a child, but she was old enough to realize that this was a life-and-death matter. She could see her grandfather's eyes, dark with fear—not the usual expression. He usually would be holding her as a treasure that he holds dear while sipping his beer with glee, but not anymore. There was a cloud of uncertainty and death lurking around them. She wondered how her parents and siblings were at this point. She thought about her fellow students, who had always been set aside as Tutsis. Would they still be alive?

A lot of hours passed as they all sat there, catching up and lamenting together. When night fell, they gave Donatha and Anne a room to stay in.

It was hard to finally sleep for the two of them. Whenever she tried to close her eyes and sleep, Donatha would see the bodies and blood-stained paths they had seen on the road earlier. Her stomach felt queasy with fear.

At some point, she fell asleep. When the morning light came and the birds chirped with happiness, all she could think of was why they were too happy about this sad world they were living in, but she rebuked herself for trying to change the course of nature.

The old man and his wife seemed to have been up for hours, as they were already eating some leftover potatoes with hot porridge when she went outside. Anne had also woken up and washed up, being fed by her grandmother, who doted on her.

"You're awake; you must be hungry. We poured your porridge; there is no sugar in it, but we are all trying." Grandma said. Donatha almost snapped. Did the old woman think everything could be solved by eating or something? She realized that she was angry at the wrong person. As a grandmother, she had no strength left to do much, so all she could do was feed her grand-daughter, at least.

That morning, for some reason, the old man woke up reading the Bible. Slim gold-rimmed glasses sat on his nose as he sat on the bench with his wife.

"This old man has decided to do some prayers and read the Bible today. I guess it's to find something to pass the time. Usually we would be feeding our animals in the barn or in the fields,preparing and preparing the land; ahaa, it's just a sad time to be alive." Grandma said,

"Grandma, I think I am full." Anne interrupted the old woman's rant.

"It's okay, dear; you will just eat the leftovers later on. Take this to Donatha; maybe she can start from here." The old woman said.

Anne found Donatha sitting in front of the hearth and handed her the plate. Before Donatha could thank her, they heard the voices of men and a woman.

"It's finally time. We are no longer going to be bribed with those silly cows and animals you give us. It's as if all isn't ours anyway." One man exclaimed.

"I think you can just take that and spare them. They're just old anyway." The woman pleaded.

"Listen to how women are foolish. A snake is a snake, whether old or young." Another man chided.

"We have offered to give you everything we have. Why would you really do this to us?" Grandpa begged the men.

Shhhh, Donatha put her finger on Anne's mouth. They peeked through a small hole that was in the wall of the kitchen, watching the whole ordeal outside.

"Yes, they are an old couple." The woman repeated.

"Would you like to die for them or with them today or something, Mukabagorora? I order you now to go back home; we will settle things here by ourselves." One man said, Donatha could see that it was her husband. Mukabagorora left in haste.

The men killed both the old man and his wife with four quick machete strikes on the head. Where Donatha and Anne hid, they only heard two breathless screams as the child's grandparents died. The reading glasses were shattered on the ground, and the Bible lay open at the feet of the men, stained with blood.

"At least they were smart to read the Bible one last time! We had been very kind to them, giving them days to live, but it looks like they were being too comfortable." One of the men bragged.

"So do we go in now and pick everything up, or can we go on and come back later?" Another man asked.

"No, let's just go. Everyone knows that the houses in this place are my conquests, so we can go and come back later to collect what they have left. We already took their cattle and money, so nothing of real value is left." Mukabagorora's husband said that and left with the second man.

After they had left, Donatha and Anne broke out into silent cries, watching the two lifeless old bodies on the ground. The old woman's head had been torn open, and the old man's was half chopped off. Donatha stormed inside, picked up the bag she had been carrying, and ran to Mukabagorora's house.

"*Egoko*! Why would you be here with a child?" Mukabagorora exclaimed when she saw them.

"Please help me; hide me; your husband just killed Anne's grandparents; we had come to hide there; he went somewhere to kill with the other man, so please just hide us for now." Donatha beseeched.

Her hands were trembling, and Anne was just there, looking horrified and in shock at what she had just seen.

"I am telling you, I have pleaded with him not to kill these old people, but of course, mercy has run out of their minds. It seems like they just want to kill." Mukabagorora said, tears running down her cheeks, crying for her husband's monstrosity. "He keeps saying that he doesn't have any mercy in him as he is not a parent."

"Just hide us, I beg of you! We'll be gone before he comes back." Donatha entreated. Finally, Mukabagorora decided to hide them in the storage room where they were packing all the things her husband had been looting from people.

All they knew was that they needed to hide, digest what had just happened, and get back on the run. "Running where and to who" was the real problem. It seemed God had forsaken people for a while.

Chapter 5

Mukabagorora ushered Donatha and Anne into the storage room, which was full of a lot of different things. There were dysfunctional house tools like wheelbarrows and construction tools, some stacked sofa sets and chairs, pieces of a dismantled queen-sized bed, and also a pile of jerrycans. They squeezed themselves among the tools and looked at Mukabagorora, who shook her head in a mixture of pity and disgust.

The two of them sat in there, unable to cry or laugh. The horrors they had just seen were hard to be sad about. It was just an instant trauma. They had smashed the old couple in less than a minute; now a child was without any family but an employee of her parent's household.

"I'm so sorry. Anne." Donatha cried, repeating the words relentlessly as if she were atoning for the sins of the monsters. At this point, all she cared about was that the child would live to tell this story; all she wanted was that the daughter of her employers would get the chance to live as she deserved. However, with the rate at which everything was happening, it was hard to tell whether anyone would survive this massacre. It was just a time like no other.

In the past, it had been bullying, sometimes scaring, and a couple of killings here and there. This time it was a full-on wipeout. It was not the government; it was not just diplomatic people involved. It was more of a virus of hatred that spread as fast as a wildfire. It didn't matter whether they knew you or not; it was as if the mere existence of the Tutsi repulsed the perpetrators. It was as if they had an itch to kill and torture; if they didn't scratch it, they would run mad. It wasn't people with power; it was their friends, childhood friends, classmates, colleagues, and so forth that were killing them. It was a strange wave of betrayal.

"I want to see my mother." Anne whispered after a long time; it was as if she had been frozen for thirty minutes, and now the aftermath of what had happened caught up with her young brain.

"I am so sorry." Donatha spoke softly, her heart breaking for the child. However, this was a situation she had no alternatives to solve. She wondered if her decision to flee to the grandparents wasn't as wise. She knew that they could die together; she had no idea whether they'd have fled. For some reason, she convinced herself that it's a good question. However, she had no other knowledge of directions or places that she could flee to.

"I want to see my mother." Anne repeated, her voice more desperate than before.

Donatha looked the child square in the eye and told her.

"I know you really want to see your parents and your brother, but I have no ability to take you to them. We're both stranded here, and I have no idea what we're going to do. All you need to know is that I will do everything in my power to make sure that you stay safe."

Anne nodded. She wasn't old, but at this point something clicked in her mind: she was alone in this world and would be with Donatha for a longer period of time. They were hiding in the house of a notorious killer; he could find them and kill them. The wife, whom she didn't know the name of, hid them, but her eyes were not kind when she did it. It looked like she was disgusted by their breathing. It was as if she was forcing herself to be nice. Or who knew? It could be a ruse that she was using to help her husband so they could kill more.

However, it seemed useless to kill her as a child, Anne thought. She didn't have any money or anything that they would take from her, nor did Donatha. They had both fled here with nothing but the small bag that Donatha came carrying. They had run here and left that behind too. They had no other clothes to wear other than the ones they were wearing; there was no hope to eat or see light again.

She mused that there was no use asking Donatha a lot of questions; she would not be able to answer them anyway. They both sat there, surrounded by a lot of materials. She wondered whether the men had been looting and storing all things in this storage. There was a pungent smell; it was as if someone had peed on a mattress that was in the corner of the room. She wondered why people would steal a mattress that was that smelly. What would they do with it? Sell it? Use it? She was baffled about how, even though they looked scary, they didn't have many brains.

However, she remembered that her mother had always told her that there was a God. She prayed the prayer in French, murmuring the words softly, hoping that it would be pleasant enough for God. Perhaps God would stop everyone who was out there to kill her or her family.

Anne and Donatha sat in the room wordlessly, each lost in their thoughts, unable to settle on a particular emotion. Donatha wondered whether her own family members, who were Hutus, hadn't started killing others. They were good and pleasant normally, but it was not a normal time. People were brutally killing and torturing those they'd known for years. Friends and even family.

Donatha commended how brave Anne was. She was the lastborn and the only daughter, so her father doted on her, but at least her mother was a voice of reason in her upbringing. Donatha remembered her words when they were in the face of death: *It's not that I will resurrect; you can kill me only once!* Perhaps she ought to adopt this behavior from now on. However, she also decided to be more prayerful this time. It was actually true that, in the face of danger, people remembered God more than ever. Neither she nor her employers were deep into religious activities, but they were all believers who went to church sometimes. She knew from different scriptures that God and Jesus were ready to protect those who were in difficulties as long as they repented of their sins and prayed for their protection.

She sat, her back to Anne, and cried to the invisible God. She wasn't sure it would work, but she had promised to protect the child within her power. She had none left in her, so the least she could do was seek the power from above.

After some time that felt like an eternity, there was some scratching on the door. It sounded like someone was opening the lock that the woman had placed in the storage room. Fearfully, Donatha stood up and approached the window. She closed her eyes and summoned all her willpower to peep through the window. It could be anyone, including Mukabagorora's husband. He was the last person she wanted to see at this moment. Yes, she had prayed for protection, but she couldn't help but be afraid for her life and Anne's.

The commotion continued; it was as if the person was struggling to get the door open. Anne and Donatha looked at each other when the wooden door squeaked open. It was Mukabagorora.

"I think they're going to come here; just hide the child inside the mattress and stand behind those bed materials; he won't be able to see you. He has already killed some people I hid before to teach me a lesson. He's not expecting me to have anyone in here. Do you understand? Do it now!" Mukabagorora whispered hurriedly.

Anne was wrapped in the pungent-smelling mattress, and Donatha hid behind the bars of the queen-sized bed. In a minute, the husband arrived.

"I need to know how many things we have collected so far. I know those little kids think that they will kill and get to have the properties; it will never happen. What I need is to be rich at the end of all this." The husband said and whistled as he stood in the storage room with his wife.

"I don't know, most of the things you stole can't be sold anywhere, you know? And what is the point of all of this?" Mukabagorora asked.

"I keep saying this: no man can succeed with the help of women. Everything you see here will be a treasure once all of this is over. A lot of things have been burned down and others destroyed; people will be buying all the essential things like chairs and mattresses." He responded, sounding pleased by the work of his hands. He started inspecting the things in the storage while Mukabagorora tried to stand in front of him to distract him.

"I know, but still, they are old and spoiled; who will buy a smelly mattress?" Mukabagorora reasoned.

"I don't think you ever support things I do. A few weeks ago, when I tried to get land from that old man, you stood up and refused to allow me to do so. I listened to you. Now that he is dead, all his things are going to be mine! He already has a lot of wealthy children out there, in Uganda and wherever, all of whom were stolen from us! Now is the time to get everything back." The husband said.

"Ahaaa,"

From where she was hiding, Donathat could see the two of them talking, and rage boiled in her stomach when she remembered how he had killed two innocent old folks. Something climbed on her feet; it felt like a spider from nowhere climbing up her legs. She tried to get it off and knocked something behind her. She was startled, but made no sound to not be even more suspicious.

"What's that in here? Let's hope you didn't bring in other people to hide; you already know that you can leave them; they will not escape us!" The husband spit down on the uncemented floor of the storage room.

"Ahaa, you're so bloodthirsty! It's just a mouse. Don't you know that this storage is rarely cleaned? They come to hide in here since it is also in the rainy season. What you did to those people has given me a lesson; I'd never hide anyone else in here." Mukabagorora said, sighed, and continued.

"You know what? The food is ready, and they have dropped a bottle of your favorite banana beer." Mukabagorora tried again when she heard a sound of things knocking over.

"Woman, are you sure that's just a mouse? Because if it's one of your other friends that you have hid in here, I will kill you first and them next." The husband snarled.

"I am not a child; I have learned my lesson. Just come with me; the food is getting cold." Mukabagorora said, ushering her husband outside the storage room.

"You women never listen; if you're that stupid to hide anyone, say goodbye to your own life. I will not keep a traitor in my house; I will not have anyone who loves these cockroaches in my room. If you side with them, you die. Are you listening to me?" The husband retorted.

"I understand you, and I love my life, so I will not do anything stupid. Now, my dear husband, shall we go eat? The food is getting cold. It's also cold weather, so I will actually put some hot water there for you to wash up." She coaxed him.

"Okay, but I will wash up later on. I want to check on some friends right after eating, so just serve me food. Bring it outside; I want to be outside." The husband retreated.

They both left after that, and all Donatha heard was the thumbs of their feet and a loud clunk when the wife locked it from outside again. She sighed deeply in relaxation. She felt like she was rightly seized in between huge fangs of death, alongside the child of her employer. In this moment, she wondered whether she would regret the decision to leave with Anne; would it have been better to leave her in the ruins of their old house? A house that was mostly filled with love and good conversation. The house that was always open for people to come and eat and ask for any other help was now a ruin. A haunted house.

Donatha wanted to scream out her frustration, her disappointment in life, and her fear of death. Unlike her, Madam, she wasn't bold enough to say that she wasn't scared of dying. She wasn't afraid to say that she had plans to survive whatever it took. That is why she was going to make these decisions.

About thirty minutes later, Mukabagorora came back and opened the door again, letting in the dim light from a rainy day. She wasn't alone, though. Donatha could hear muffled voices discussing something while she and Anne remained in their hiding spot.

"You can come out now, Donatha. Come here." Mukabagorora said, her voice bitter and almost reincarnating the same vehemence against Tutsi her husband had.

"Thank you so much for hiding the both of us. I really don't know what we should do from now on because your husband is very serious and bloodthirsty; he wouldn't hesitate to kill us all and have us pulled into the pits that they've dug." Donatha said, her heart swelling with hatred, anger, and fear.

"It's good that you know that I helped you. I don't know what you are expecting from me, but dying for you is not going to happen." Mukabagorora said fiercely, clenching her jaw. The woman behind her sneered a bit but said nothing about the situation.

"Please try a bit more. Please try to hide us a bit more." Donatha spoke, her eyes wistful. Anne hid behind her, warily watching the two women in front of her.

"There is no way that I can hide you in here any longer. I only have one plan; if it doesn't work out, you'll have to fend for-" Mukabagorora stopped in her speech.

"Don't worry about me. At least if you can't hide the both of us, just hide this child. She deserves to live a bit more. Please." Donatha cried and dropped to her knees. "I swear she has a rich family in Belgium; if the child survives, the relatives will give you a lot of money once all of this ends."

"Ah, if that's the case, then I know what we're going to do. Donatha, you go into the bush nearby; I will not let anyone go near that bush. This child will go with my sister; they live nearby, so it would be easy to check on her from time to time when the men are on a break or are too drunk to do anything. My sister and I wouldn't mind making more money, especially in the times when all of this is finally over, though I can't tell when this will end." Mukabagorora concluded.

Donatha looked at Anne in despair; she had no other ways to save this child unless she sent her to some last-minute saviors who were not even doing this out of kindness but for money. She tried to console herself with the thought that she was Mukabagorora's sister, who was alert and happy when they mentioned her name in the deal. Her expression mirrored that of a cat that captures a handful of mice.

"If you agree, my husband just stepped out with his friends. This is the time to do it. Almost everyone that you will pass by knows my husband and respects what he says. Whoever stops them, tell them to let you go. As for you, Donatha, I suppose you will have to do with the bush. You're a grown up, plus your features betray you already; there is no way to even hide you." Mukabagorora announced. Anne was pulled out of the storage and taken away without even a last hug or handshake.

"Come with me." Mukabagorora said, "I will go inside and fetch some more garments for you to use while you're in the bush. Am I not doing God's work here?" Mukabagorora spoke, more to herself than to Donatha.

Donatha watched the other woman race into her house and left her outside. A bloodied machete was leaning on the wall outside; there was also a space that had some dried blood and dirt on it. She felt fear creep up her spine. How sure was she that the woman was just luring her out for her husband to slaughter? She had to trust the process. It wasn't as if beggars couldn't be choosers. Only in a fairytale, this time was nothing like a fairytale but rather like being trapped in a horror movie.

In a minute, Mukabagorora emerged from the mud house with a pile of clothing and fabric. She handed them to Donatha, who was overwhelmed by the warmth; after all, she had nothing covering her. For a split second, she was almost grateful, but she remembered that Anne had left without enough things to warm her. How was she going to cope with the cold weather, and what if they tortured her instead of safely hiding her?

"These are all I can find; let me go find some bags made of our polyethylene so that you have a place to keep them when it rains. Actually, if it rains, there is an old toilet that we no longer use; it's covered, though." Mukabagorora explained and went in pursuit of the polyethylene bag.

Once all was settled, Donatha was escorted to the bush where she was supposed to hide. What the other woman hadn't mentioned was that the bush was literally on the side of the path that the folks in the neighborhood passed by to the small tap where they fetched water.

"You hadn't told me that it was this bush you were referring to." Donatha exclaimed in disappointment.

"This is safer than you are thinking. I know firsthand that unless they know you're in there, which I will not tell a soul, they would never think that someone is hiding in that obvious place." Mukabagorora reassured.

The last thing Donatha felt was relief. This was worse than remaining at the ruins of Anne's grandparents. However, that was a danger zone too, since they'd need to go there to loot and destroy everything. At this point, she had no choice but to just go straight into the bush, pray, and hope for the best.

"I'm taking my leave then. I will see you tomorrow when he's not here. I will bring you food." Mukabagorora said and grinned as if happy that she still possessed some humanity in her. Donatha was thankful to God that she and Anne had temporary shelter until some time they didn't know.

Donatha sat behind the bush; luckily, she noticed a plan with thorns before she laid down. She uprooted it and kept it near to be able to use it as a weapon to deter anyone who wanted to touch her. She decided that whoever would kill her in the future would also be left with a scratch or, better yet, a wound.

As dusk started to set in, Donatha had dozed off but was awoken by the sounds of girls whispering in hushed voices near the bush. At least they weren't killers.

I think right now they're going to gather soon; they gather right when it darkens. I don't know what time it is, to be honest. One woman said.

But how are you sure that they actually come every night? Another queried.

I know because one of my friends was hiding right in this bush. She hid in here for a long time, just from the beginning of this whole nightmare. She had heard the men come down, she told me, but apparently, not only did she know that they pass by every night, they also suspected there was someone in here. She was killed the next day, and they had all raped her. The first woman explained, *So, let's go. I heard these men are looking for beautiful girls to keep in their houses too.*

Donatha continued to listen to the conversation, but the deeper they went, the more terrified she was.

They then took her and many other people to throw them into some of the pits they had dug. The first woman continued. *But if we make it there before them. We can try to talk to them and see how it goes, right?*

I understand. Let's go then. What would we do anyway? Our families that fled—didn't we hear that they all died anyway? Another third voice spoke

Donatha wondered how many of them were there. She also wanted to know what they would do when the men actually came. One suspicion she had was confirmed already. This bush wasn't a hideout; it was even worse. She doubted Mukabagorora hadn't heard about that person killed in the bush on their land. She, of course, knew, but decided to bait her.

After the women had left, she decided that she was going to follow them closely and see whether she'd do as they would to get saved. To this point, she had no idea what their plan to survive was, but it had to work. If it didn't work, she would have done her best; only God could dictate destiny to work in her favor or not.

She followed slowly in their tracks, especially since the path was slippery with mud. She had brought along the clothes in the bag that she had gotten; who knew when they would come in handy?

The woman reached a place around the tap where they all hid behind big rocks, which Donatha emulated. As if on cue, three men arrived with spears and machetes, and they put them in the stream of stagnant water around the tap to clean the blood off. Donatha watched with fear, wondering whether the women had thought about this plan clearly before they admitted to doing it.

The men also had some bags; they removed different things, generally money and other valuables. They counted their money and laughed out loud at how much they had been able to loot in one day. They bragged about how, even though they weren't big initiators of the killings, they were given the job of throwing people away and finishing others off. They joked about the people they'd left for the dead.

All of a sudden, the women started to rise from behind the stones; Donatha didn't do the same right away. The men reached for their weapons as well and asked the girls if they'd like to have fun before they killed them.

One of the women spoke first: *How about we make a deal, though? How about you choose whoever you like among us and take us with you? We'll do everything you want us to do, and we will please you.*

The men laughed hard and asked them how they were daring enough to suggest such a thing, but eventually the men gave into temptation. Donatha realized that perhaps the womans ruse would work out alright. She thanked God for the darkness that covered her and the men were focused on the other girls. She also appeared and stood there.

One man reached for her. He stared at her intensely; she couldn't tell whether he wanted to see her better or not. The man removed something from his pocket and used a small flashlight that was on a lighter to look at her better. He studied her face more; everyone's attention was on her.

"What's your name?" The man asked.

"Donatha." She replied in a quivering voice.

"Don't be afraid, alright. I am a murderer, but I also love beautiful girls." He touched her cheek, and she moved her face away, which caused a ripple of laughter from the men.

"I like them shy. Guy, I think each one of you should take two each; I have found one of my own." The guy announced. He fancied her from what she could tell. This was a good thing. At least she would go with one man. He wasn't bad-looking either; it was a pity he was even a murderer. His face showed strength and ruggedness, but not the bad kind, but rather the type that should invoke a sort of assurance in a person.

"I like them young and shy. I will take you. I actually live nearby too, so it won't take me long to get you home and savor you to the fullest." He said and grinned.

The next thing she knew, her hand was in his, and he dragged her behind him. She couldn't tell what the girls thought since none of them spoke again. They evidently didn't want the men to back down on their decision. Donatha wondered how this idea had actually worked.

Not that she was happy with the thought of being raped by a random guy, but she hoped she would find a way to escape him before they reached where he claimed was his house.

On their way, Donatha prayed hard for God to make a way, but still her conscience gnawed at her: What would she do against this burly man, who wasn't also too big? She would run, she'd catch her, she'd scream, and she would alert more killers to feast on her and finish her off. For now, she'd follow this murderer, who's a total stranger, and wait for God to work in mysterious ways.

Chapter 6

Anne looked around the room they had put her in. The room smelled of stale urine, and she suspected that the pungent smell was emanating from the mattress. There was a clothesline above that crossed the tiny room. The clothes hanging on it were small, as if there were babies or young children who stayed in the room. It was strange because she hadn't seen any children her age or younger since she came.

The only information she had was that Donatha was hiding somewhere in the bush, and the woman she was with now was the sister of a woman whose husband killed her grandparents. The very thought of it made her want to puke and cry at the same time. She was traumatized. She couldn't help but wonder where her lovely mother and her strong father were. What had become of her brothers? She had no idea.

She also wondered where her friend Jeph's family was. She had a lot of questions—too many questions. The dark was falling outside, and the room was darkening as well. She had never had to stay in such shabby and terrifying conditions as she had the past week. She was, at least, grateful that Donatha was still with her. She was the only familiar face, and now she too was nowhere to be seen.

All of a sudden, she heard the voices of people. Some people were coming into the house. The baritone laughter sounded sinister, even muffled by the mud wall between the room and the living room. A chirpy voice greeted them and offered food. It must be the sister, Anne thought to herself. She also heard some cries; it sounded like a baby.

It was a baby.

The door opened, and the sister stood in the door clutching the baby against her hip. The smell of urine was even stronger. Anne wondered whether the woman had lost her sense of smell or had acclimated to the unsanitariness of their house, and particularly of this room.

"We have a child of your age, Marebe; she will give you some of her clothes to wear while you are here. Now go ahead and remove those fancy clothes. They told me that your parents were rich, but no one needs to know about that. If anyone asks you over dinner, don't say your name; just pretend to be deaf and mute. Do you hear me?" The woman ordered.

Remove my fancy clothes; these aren't even my best. You should have seen the dress my dad brought me last Christmas, Anne thought. *These people are so bitter, they don't even want me to say my name.*

"Have you heard what I said, or do you actually have difficulties listening in normal life?" The woman nearly barked.

Okay, madam, I have heard you; life is already hard; shouting at me will not bring me my family; I have no idea about their whereabouts. Anne nearly snorted.

"Yes, I understand." She replied, pretending to be meek and understanding while all she wanted was to roll her eyes at her. Her parents had taught her that elders always deserve to be respected, even if they're in the wrong. Don't use any reactions that would seem disrespectful.

"Dinner will be served in ten minutes; be ready, come into the room, and greet everyone you will find there without a word. If you don't do as I order, you might just get killed. I guess you're not a stranger to dying and the concept of killing by now." The woman said and exited the room.

Why would anyone do this? These people will be burned in hell for sure. Anne mused.

Her parents had always taught her that everything done without love is a crime and a sin. People should always love each other, even when they have disagreements. However, it seemed that perhaps not everyone followed that rule. She had started to feel different at school; every child at her former school was from a well-off family, but some hated each other. Most of them hated her and some other students. They said the Tutsis were cockroaches and snakes; they pulled bad pranks on them, some of which she had told her parents.

Her parents, especially her father, treated her as a princess. He said that everyone should be able to see that she's a bright young girl with a promising future; anyone thinking otherwise would be wrong. Anne wasn't sure she had a bright future ahead of her anymore.

She had lost family; she was with people who killed, people who slaughtered people, like how their former houseguard used to slaughter chickens or goats when there was a party. She wasn't sure how this happened, regardless of whether it was happening.

Realizing that the woman had been serious, disobeying the woman's orders might get her killed too. These people had killed her grandparents without thinking twice or even accusing them of anything concrete other than who they were. Disobeying would result in even worse things.

Anne stepped out of her garments; she rummaged through the woven basket with a lot of clothes and ended up picking the most tidy-looking dress and putting it on. It smelled like urine, too. She was starting to wonder whether these people washed their clothes with urine as well. Regardless, she put it on and stepped out into the tiny living room.

Three men and a girl, whom Anne assumed was Marebe, were holding a baby whose face was smeared with a mixture of mud, food, and mucus from her nose.

Gross, Anne thought, *these people have no manners or decency at all.*

She greeted everyone, and chills ran down her spine when one of the men held her hand a little longer, perusing her face. For once, Anne liked the terrifying woman, who quickly interjected and pried her away from the man.

"She's my sister's niece; she's staying with us for now. You know how things are these days; she can't handle all the children; they mostly send them to her when they're not going to school." The woman said, "Marebe, take Simbi out at the back to get your food, and don't interrupt us; no child should sit like that amongst older people."

The man's eyes were still fixated on her when Anne followed Marebe, who was struggling to hold the baby on her; rightly so, the baby was big, plumb, and wiggly all through. She didn't want to leave her mother.

"Marebe, leave the baby here. Just go with Simbi; eat from the backdoor." The woman finally said. Anne sighed, so her name was going to be Simbi from today, Simbi, who was also deaf and mute.

***

On the way, the killer didn't talk to her; he just held her hand in a deadly tight grip and pulled her along with him. He had a fast pace, which had her panting by the time they reached the killers' house.

Outside, a number of bloodied weapons had been left there; it seemed like they had been there for some time since the rain had washed off the blood, leaving a stain on the ground. Donatha shuddered at the thought of what this man was going to do to her.

To her surprise, when they were in the confines of the house, which seemed like no one had lived there for a long time, the man's expression softened. Still mute, he poured something that looked like banana juice, *umutobe*, and handed the cup to her before pouring himself one too.

"Where are you from, and how did you get here?" He asked quietly as he sipped his own drink.

Shocked, Donatha responded, "My birthplace is here, but I had gone to work as a maid in the city; by God's will, I managed to flee, though it hasn't helped me at all."

"Okay. What about your family or your employers?" He queried. His expression was almost too innocent to be that of a murderer.

"I have no idea where they are. Why are you pretending to be nice? Just get it over with." Donatha said, seething with anger about his double faces. He was a killer, a murderer, and a rapist who looted as well. Why was he asking all of this, just so he could track them down and kill them?

"My name is Jean, and trust me, I never ever thought I would kill; just before all this started, I had never even slaughtered an animal. I actually have never killed anyone; I just strike them and leave them for my friends to finish off." He said, his expression almost somber.

Donatha couldn't believe her ears. Did he think she would squeal and congratulate him on that? She shot him a deadly glare.

"I am only being honest; back at the river, I had no choice but to pick up a girl; you don't understand! If I don't kill, they'll kill me." He confessed. Donatha had no sympathy for him. He had chosen to stand with evil, to kill, rape, and loot; he didn't get the grace of empathy.

"I don't care; you have hurt people who are only as innocent as you. I am not a genius, but everyone knows that this is the devil's work, and you're simply carrying it out. I'm sure there are other Hutus who aren't killing. It's a choice, and you should know that this won't last forever; you will not wipe away everyone!" Donatha shouted at him.

Jean put his cup down and got up to leave.

"Just go in the other small room to see if there is something you can eat; if you want to sleep, I have a blanket and a mat, *umusambi*, for you. There is also a torch with batteries; I am taking this one with me. Don't wait up for me." he said, standing in the doorway and left.

Confused was an understatement. Jean looked about her age or younger, but she couldn't find it in her heart to sympathize with him. Yes, he was young and afraid for his life, so he decided to join the bad people. He didn't get to be pitied; what was pitiful were the people he killed, the girls he raped, and the people he had displaced from their properties.

That night, Donatha struggled to fall asleep. How was Anne? What had become of her parents? The sight of Anne's grandparents being slaughtered haunted her. She prayed and cried for herself, the people she knew, and the country until she fell asleep.

For the next week or so, Jean would leave home with a machete or the small gun he kept. She suspected that the gun had no more bullets left, which is why he left it at home. He would come back with food, typically meat, and a bloodied machete or club.

He didn't speak with him more than a hello and a good night; however, true to his word, he didn't touch her at all; he never even requested her to sleep with him. Each time, he ate by himself in the room, which he insisted she should never go into. Every time their gazes met, he was filled with guilt and fear. Each night, he seemed more weary than the previous day.

Until one fateful night, when he came in and said,.

"They want to take you away from me and kill you." Jean said.

"What? Who?" Donatha burst out.

"My other friends said that they think I have been intentionally keeping you to myself; they too want to savor you, or they will kill us both if I refuse. In their words, 'When a snake coils around a butter churn, igisabo, you have no choice but to break it too.'" Jean replied.

"What will you do?" Donatha asked, tears stinging her eyes. The inevitable was coming. To be in a war was one thing; to be a woman in a war, however, was the worst-case scenario.

"I am not sure yet. I told them that the maximum lengths I would go to were to allow them to be in the house while we slept together." Jean said.

"What?" Donatha queried. Considering the gravity of the situation, Jean was trying to do his best. Unfortunately, his best was still a horrible action.

"I have no choice, and you need to understand that I have committed a lot of crimes already, but given that you and I have been technically living together, I really wouldn't want to hurt you. I appreciate how to cook, clean, and stay patient." Jean said, his tone melancholic.

Donatha wanted to shout at him that she wasn't here on her own will, but again, that would be being ingrate considering that she had prayed to God for protection and for weeks she had been very safe with Jean. Minus the terror of not knowing how Anne was and the sight of blood every single day.

"I'm sorry, Jean; I don't have the heart to be grateful right now. I can't be happy when I know what you're doing, but I also can't thank you enough for keeping me safe." Donatha said, tears trickling down her cheek. Jean reached out and wiped away the tears softly. Donatha was surprised that one person could be both monstrous and kind. It was a complicated matter.

"I wish things were different. I wish I wasn't a man who kills and loots. I wish there was no war, I wish there was peace, and I wish I had known you before you left to search for work when we were still young. I like your nature; you say things that you feel, and you have never lied about being grateful. Whatever will happen, I am not sure, but thank you for making me think about myself." Jean said.

Donatha cried without reserving herself. She had said that he was not pitiful, but at this moment, they were two humans on extreme ends, two victims, with one who had transformed himself into a villain to survive. Who would take the blame?

***

Anne had grown accustomed to the pungent smell of the room, porridge without sugar, and eating sweet potatoes for breakfast, lunch, and dinner. Even the howling of the men when they talked about their conquests of how the day's work had been really bad, when they bragged about how many people they each had killed. To date, she hadn't been able to know who was Mama Marebe's husband; all the men touched her, and they took turns going into the bedroom. She wasn't too young to know what men and women did in their rooms because the house was very small. Sometimes she heard screams, and it most certainly wasn't the baby, because the baby slept with them most of the time. Now she understood why everything reeked of urine. Marebe was too young to wash all the clothes nicely, and the baby wasn't old enough to not pee on the bed, and since it was in a rainy season, they mostly had to sleep on the bed as it is.

She hadn't stopped thinking about her family or Donatha, despite the life she was leading as a mute. However, she sometimes bantered with Marebe or spoke with her. Marebe had big, sad eyes full of pain and tiredness. The girl looked and behaved like she was very old. She had no wish to play, and even when Anne tried to ask her about herself, the girl spoke little to no words.

One afternoon, the men came home early, and Mama Marebe greeted them with calabashes full of banana beer, urwagwa. They sat down, but not as cheerfully as usual. One of the men still wielded his bloodied machete.

"Why couldn't you leave it outside?" Mama Marebe exclaimed.

"Because I might need to use it right now." The man retorted, and the woman recoiled. Goosebumps formed on Anne's arms.

"What do you mean you might need to use it?" She queried, "Have I stopped feeding you and sleeping with you?"

"But you lied. There is nothing worse than parading a cockroach in front of us every single day, calling her a different name, pretending that she's deaf, which she can hear and talk to, and is not your sister's niece but a rich cockroach you're planning to make money off of." The man said it with such vehemence that it made his veins stand alert on his face.

Anne shuddered. *Who told these men all about me?*

When Mama Marebe said nothing, the man spat in her face. "You're such an idiot; did you think your sister wouldn't rattle on you? She's older, but dumber. We're taking the kid anyway; you're just lucky you're our own kind; otherwise, I'd strike my machete on your lying neck so you'd never do it again!"

Taking the kid? Anne winced. *This can't be true; where are they taking me?*

"I can explain everything; it's not like I would eat the money alone; she has very rich relatives; we need to have her safe; that's why I wanted to hide her at first." Mama Marebe pleaded, but to no avail, because the man yanked Anne to his side and told his fellows that he had a plan.

"Here is where we're going to go; if this kid has rich parents, they probably speak French, and if we keep her here with this good-for-nothing woman, we lose. I propose we send her to Jean's house. He has a secluded place, not a whorehouse like here; he also speaks some French, which means that when those people come, he will be our interpreter." The man laughed out loud, happy for the plan he had just devised on the spot.

The other men nodded their heads; Mama Marebe seethed with anger but said nothing. Anne looked back and forth amongst men, and in her heart, she prayed to be safe. How it would go, she had no idea.

In the short stained dress borrowed from Marebe, she followed the men, who had their machetes and clubs propelled against their shoulders as they sang that they would cleanse out all the Tutsi along the way.

As they walked, there was a bush nearby that was moving. Two of the men told one to hold Anne as they ran after the people who had been in the bush—a young boy and his mother. It didn't take them two minutes to slide their necks and stab them multiple times before pulling their bodies farther into the bush.

Anne closed her eyes. Since her grandparent's death, she hadn't seen any other brutal killings. On their way, they crossed what looked like an ambush or a lot of young men with all sorts of weapons; they exchanged a few words, and they continued. They also passed by men and women who were dragging dead bodies into pits or transporting them there.

How no one questioned them was a surprise to her. She thought that perhaps the men who were kidnapping her were influential in their area because everyone seemed to respect them. No wonder though; their faces were scared and scary, very dark with forever scowls and frowns.

How far will we go, though? Anne wondered as she panted a few hours later. She was thirsty and hungry, but she wouldn't dare say a thing. At some point, she noticed that they were in the same neighborhood as where her grandparents used to live. It seemed like she would always spiral back to the most horrific event of her life.

"So, we're almost there. Jean mentioned that he still has the woman living with him, and right now, I am very happy that he ended up not killing her. We need to take special care of this kid;

since she has some relatives who are white, they will reward us for protecting her thus far." One of the men said.

"Let's leave her with Jean, but we can't fully trust him. He's such a wimp sometimes; we'll have to always come back and check how she's doing." Another said.

"You're definitely right; all of us just don't have the stability of somewhere to hide the girl; he's our last resort!" Another exclaimed.

Who's Jean? Anne pondered, *Is he a nice guy at least? Won't he kill me?*

After a few more minutes, they reached.

***

After learning that the men wanted to watch Jean rape her, Donatha felt like she wasn't sure about what to do, and Jean seemed like he was trying his best not to do it either.

He was outside listening to the radio, with the songs inciting and encouraging the extermination of Tutsis on air. Sometimes they'd give commentaries that were downright hateful. There was no more hiding; the radio was now a tool to drive the war forward and kill as many Tutsis as possible.

All of a sudden, Donatha heard voices outside, and she went to check through the window. It was three men and a girl; she noticed her at first, *Anne*. Fear ran through her veins. *How did Anne meet these killers, even with their bloody machetes in hand?*

"Hi Jean, we never thought we would do this, but here we are; the gamble is too good." One of the men started. "We discovered a treasure from our whore. This kid has rich families; some relatives are even white, and I am sure they speak French. We have decided that you're the most stable one suitable to keep the child with the other woman. Where is she anyway? I'd like to sample her too!"

The other men, other than Jean, burst out laughing at his last sentence. Donatha wished she could borrow a few minutes of power, kill all of them, and flee with Anne.

"Ahaa, what's the proof that you have a rich child? Or even if she is, how will you be able to meet these relatives? Did you think about when they would come?" Jean asked seriously, which gloomied the faces of the men. It was as if they hadn't thought about all those details before. They had just heard of rich relatives and grew wings automatically.

"We never thought about that before, but there should be a way to get to the relatives. Whether soon or later, rich and white people will come for their child. We shall be in possession of the child until then." One of the men said, to which all the others nodded.

"Alright, just leave her here, but here is the thing: if you guys want me to keep the baby safe, she's still the enemy, so you won't tell anyone about it at all; otherwise, we too would be killed for being ibyisto, the accomplices!" Jean urged the men.

"Well, that is true; we'll keep her here until we get our money. We'll be leaving shortly then." The men said and left.

Donatha, who was watching through the curtains, was filled with so much joy that she was seeing Anne alive and well. She ran outside and hugged her strongly. The child seemed as shocked as she was as well. God truly works in mysterious ways. One could never know how God did things. Not a hair off of her beautiful head, Anne looked at Donatha, then Jean, with a myriad of questions in her expression.

"Well, Donatha, I am happy that you know the child, so at least I can do all I can to save two people." Jean said. He had been melancholic throughout the day, and Donatha certainly didn't want to pity him whatsoever.

"Thanks for accepting to help us." Donatha thanked him with her eyes still misty. Whatever had grown between the two of them over the past few weeks was to be forbidden. It wasn't worth it.

"I have learned that Inkotanyi has started to take over the majority of the places; people are fleeing and killing at the same time, and we don't want to pay for our crimes. Tomorrow, I will inquire with everyone I know and see if we can flee here and reach the zones that have been captured by Inkotanyi. I am willing to give myself up." Jean said.

Donatha realized that perhaps some of these killers were also victims of bad governance and time. She had never asked Jean more about himself, but he seemed like a well-mannered young man; evidently, he was also educated because he spoke French as well. The biggest question was how he had ended up becoming a murderer.

"Why would you do this for us?" Donatha asked.

"I am as much of a victim; I have never wanted to become the monster I am today. If the country has started to be taken over by sane people, I am willing to give up. I am willing to save you for sure." Jean responded.

Donatha cooked a nice meal of rice, meat, and some potatoes for Anne and Jean. She served some leftover banana juice that was starting to go sour as well.

Jean and Donatha slept together, a little bit happy that they had been able to reconnect.

The next day, Donatha attempted to fetch some vegetables from the nearby bushes because they had finished the meal the previous night. Jean had stayed home with Anne alone.

"So Anne, your parents are wealthy, I heard." Jean started. Anne watched him. His expression wasn't as innocent as it had been the day earlier, but she didn't mind. He was their savior at the moment.

"Not as much as people assume, but my father was a business-man; my mother worked in the ministry." Anne said.

"That's good to know. You're such a beautiful girl anyway." Jean grinned, and chills went down Anne's spine. They were in the small mud house together, alone, without Donatha to talk to. All of a sudden, danger felt close to home.

"I have brought you from these bad people, so do you want to remove your clothes and show me how you look without them?" Jean asked.

"Why do you want me to remove my clothes?"

"So that I can look at your beautiful, small body." Jean said, grabbing her arm. He pushed her small body on the mat covered with the blanket and started to remove his own clothes in a rush.

"What do you want to do to me? Please don't!" Anne cried in terror when he swung his manhood out of his pants. Anne had never thought she would see the male genitalia of a grown man before. Jean did not stop.

Behind the seemingly remorseful killer lay a pedophile with no mercy.

As he took her, Anne tried to cry, but he muffled the screams with his large hand. Anne had never felt the same pain in her entire life. Blood stained the blanket, and tears dampened the little dress she had on. When he was done, Jean sighed!

"Fresh and young, just how I prefer them!" He laughed. "If you say anything, I won't just do it this once; I will do it to both you and Donatha, and then I will ask the other men to kill you and cut you slowly so that you will feel the pain!"

"Please don't kill me!" Anne cried. "I will not say anything."

Jean cleaned her thighs in a hurry with the blanket, then he went to the small room, cut his own hand, and cleaned himself on the blanket. Donatha would not differentiate his blood from Anne's. Anne would avoid Donatha, but she would curl herself up and cry.

The following days were characterized by them fleeing the spot in which they had been hiding and traveling long distances to meet the RPF, a journey on which they met Aunt Costa, who'd been living in Uganda for a long time. Aunt Costa thanked Jean and paid him for keeping her niece alive. Anne lived through that; she did not say a word. What had happened to her was buried in a drawer of her heart, which she would never open any time soon, to anyone.

Aunt Costa was a wealthy woman who had built businesses from scratch; a woman who supported her family as much as she could, and there and then, she decided to take in Anne.

A child who didn't know whether she was an orphan or not; a child who had seen people getting killed; a child raped by a temporary savior; and a child who had survived one of the worst things on the planet. A Genocide.

The 1994 Genocide Against the Tutsi.

Part 2: Debris

Chapter 7

Can a person transition from fearing for life for every single second to being happy? Can a person forget the horrors that spanned months? Can a person forget bloodstained machetes and gunfire?

People who'd lived in a closely knit society were now finding themselves navigating the somber remnants of a community shattered by unspeakable violence. The violence was incited by numerous hidden agendas. The propaganda that had started decades ago, the libellous speeches that had been shared in public spaces, and the training given to civilians to turn them into an army of darkness had finally ended in genocide. An ethnic cleansing activity.

Would it have been easier to be killed by other strangers from far away, or death is death however it happens? While some were killed by people they didn't know, many were killed by their neighbors, friends, and colleagues. How could one move beyond that kind of betrayal? How could they unsee their own people die because of who they were born from?

Survivors filled the streets, barefoot and thirsty. Thirsty for the familiar faces they used to see across the street, in the markets, in buses, at work; however, all those familiar faces were now pieces of body parts discarded by killers all around the country: on the roadsides, in pits, in rivers, in lakes, in churches, in schools.

How were they supposed to realize who had been their mothers, fathers, relatives, and friends when the killers had dismantled their bodies with guns, grenades, and machetes? Agahinda ntikica kagira mubi. Grief doesn't kill; it makes one ugly. Literally.

Buildings, old and in colonial style, were marked with scars of the genocide; the ruins were painful and piercing like a spear. Some were dilapidated with marks of bullets, like they refused to give up, like they wanted to remain standing, waiting for the survivors to make them makeshift shelters. Some places are untouched but haunting to everyone who would attempt to step into them.

Some people are always luckier than others. While some people had somewhere to lay their heads at night, others had their houses set on fire, their properties looted by the perpetrators, and upon coming back, they had nowhere to go. While the RPA had managed to support them with food and other essentials, they couldn't help millions and millions of people resettle into their lives with all that a person needs to survive.

The biggest quest was, how would a broken heart be mended? How would the traumatized brains be healed? It wasn't possible to completely fill the holes of loss in their lives. It was all about starting from scratch, starting from ruins, and starting to build a community of people who weren't able to withstand what their eyes had seen.

Some lost their limbs and had fatal head wounds, and some others weren't able to face reality anymore. How would a society like that be built again?

It would definitely take patience, forgiveness, and an immense amount of resilience.

Anne, eight years old and unharmed physically, was rescued alongside Donatha. She didn't have much information about what had happened or what caused it, but there was no longer a child or an adult involved in the tragedy. It is true that people mature with danger, not years. She had grown up in the comfort of a loving family. A loving family that didn't have a clue of its whereabouts. She dearly missed her father and mother. She had gone from being the princess of the house to an unofficial orphan.

Donatha was her heroine. Nights in the bush, walking and carrying Anne on her back, she would never forget how she had stayed with her since the entire ordeal started until the end. Donatha always prioritized Anne's life over hers; she made sure that she was safe or with people that she could be somewhat safe with. She still treated her like a princess through the hard times. Sometimes, even though Anne didn't say anything, she thought about Donatha's family. Where were they? She knew from the stories they shared in her home's kitchen that she had cousins, aunts, and uncles, but amid the entire genocide, Donatha never brought them up. Anne wondered if it was to avoid hurting her or scaring her further. She was always worried about why the woman never once showed her weaknesses. Even on the first night, when their house guard came with men with machettes and tried to rape her, she never faltered. She upheld her dignity.

Dignity and regalness reminded Anne of her mother. Where was she? Where was her father? They'd left with the neighbor and never came back. She hadn't heard from them. It's been a long time now. She couldn't tell which day or date it was anymore. She used to know days and dates because of school. Would she ever go back to school? Were her friends and teachers still alive, or had they been killed too?

When RPA rescued her and Donatha, Jean, the man who had tried to hide them and then raped her, was also taken because he was also a perpetrator. A few days later, she met Aunt Costa. Aunt Costa resembled her father so much. Tall, slender, and soft but firm spoken. She had beautiful hair coiffed in a tight ponytail. It surprised Anne because it seemed that everyone else they met was very disheveled. Reasonably so, who had time to do their hair amid the killings? Everyone was worried about whether they'd see another day with their families or friends; no one had time to think about beauty. The ugliness of death shadowed any type of beauty.

Aunt Costa also had access to a car that would take Anne and her, along with other people, back to Kigali. She had never seen Aunt Costa before other than hearing her in family stories and hearing that she lived in Kampala and Mbarara most of the time. However, her mannerisms were exactly like those of her father. She was a voice of reason and hope at the same time. She seemed ruthless from afar, though. Anne concluded.

The only sad fact was that Anne had to leave Donatha behind. Her excuse was that she needed to also find her family. Anne understood what she meant but was sad nonetheless. She'd hoped they'd stay together some more time. It wasn't possible.

Once they hopped into the backseat of the car, Anne was almost afraid of looking at Aunt Costa. She had once been a very proactive child, but the coldness in her heart rendered her speechless. She'd seen too much in such a short period of time. Every time she wanted to speak, nothing came out. As if Aunt Costa could tell, she started the conversation in French.

"So, Anne, I haven't been able to know what we'll do yet, but we need to get you somewhere safer. In Kigali, I have a house near what used to be your home; that's where we'll be staying." Aunt Costa said.

Silence. A minute, two. Anne gazed outside the revving car, the dirt roads starting to get dry from the rainy season. She decided to lower the glass on her side of the window. The air was filled with a stench that she couldn't decipher, so she closed the window again.

"Did you hear me?" Aunt Costa asked softly.

Silence. A minute.

"Yes, Aunt. I heard you." Anne finally responded.

"So, right now, I am the family you have; please talk to me about any kind of problem you might be having. Is that okay?" Aunt Costa coaxed.

Silence.

"Yes, Aunt. I understand."

It wasn't comprehending that was hard for Anne; it was the responding part that seemed laborious. Was she supposed to be happy that she would be living in the same village and neighborhood that she had grown up in without her parents and favorite neighbors? It wouldn't be the same. Every single day would be a pain to remember her happy times in this place.

"Are you not happy that we are going to be together? I still have no information about what happened to your parents and brothers, but I at least found you! That's all I can ask for. I am deeply indebted to Donatha for keeping you safe all this time." Aunt Costa said, on the verge of tears. Her voice broke, invoking a stare from the driver, who'd been focused on the road since they entered.

The man reached into the passenger seat and gave her a hand-kerchief, which Aunt Costa accepted and mumbled, thanks to which the man nodded wordlessly. Anne looked back and forth from the driver to Aunt Costa, who dabbed at her eyes.

"Thank you." Anne mumbled. Even though she didn't want to say much, she recognized the sacrifice that Aunt Costa had made, traveling amid the tragedy to find her. She could imagine the trouble she went through to find her.

She wasn't ungrateful; she just didn't know how to do this. How was she supposed to respond like the princess she'd been? A golden child who responded with unmatched politeness had all older people love her and set her as an example.

At this point, she was just a perplexed child.

"I didn't get to see grandpa and grandma, and I didn't have a conversation with Donatha to figure out where they might be right now. The car couldn't wait for us until we found them." Aunt Costa said.

Don't scream. Anne thought to herself. This was a memory she'd pushed down into her core. It was a box of literally dead bodies that Aunt Costa wanted to open up again.

"Did you ever meet up with them? I remember well that they lived in the vicinity of where I found you and Donatha." Aunt Costa asked again.

Anne looked outside again, letting her brain wander to the trees and the bushes instead of that wretched morning.

"I did," Anne replied at last. "They were killed."

Aunt Costa's breath hitched, but her eyes didn't tear up.

The machetes, the bible, the blood—it all came rushing into Anne's brain, but she didn't say a word. Her beloved grandparent had been slaughtered, right in front of her eyes. Such kind and prayerful people. She couldn't understand why their neighbors would want to murder them that brutally.

"I didn't know. We don't have to talk about it now. We need to reach Kigali first." Aunt Costa said.

Anne sighed in relief. These memories don't have space in the present. They were to be inside her forever; she wouldn't talk about it.

"I have three children—two girls and a boy—at home. I hope you will be close to them. They're closer to your age, so don't worry, you won't be alone anymore." Aunt Costa consoled her.

"I wasn't alone before. I was with Donatha." Anne refuted, her tone calm but hiding rage inside.

"I didn't mean it like that. I meant people who are in your family. My children are your cousins; you will be together." Aunt Costa explained.

"They're not my brothers, and you're not my parents, either." Anne shouted at her aunt.

Silence filled the car.

"I'm sorry, Aunt. I didn't mean to be disrespectful." Anne amended.

Aunt Costa could tell that this was a child bruised by the past. This was a child with a lot of hurt and confusion bottled up in her heart. It wasn't her fault that politics was a nasty game that led people to kill their neighbors remorselessly. Anne needed just some time to heal. Much like everyone who'd witnessed these horrors.

Perhaps once she was back in Kigali, where she grew up, she'd come back to her senses. She'd be somewhat familiar with the terrain. She'd be more comfortable. Or Aunt Costa hoped so.

The journey back to Kigali took longer than Anne had hoped it would be. It felt like it had been ages since she'd been here. The last time she'd been on these roads, there were roadblocks all the way, and now there were stains of blood on the grass and roads. Dilapidated houses and facilities. Holes on some, smoke stains on others.

She wondered whether their house had also been burned or shot through. Would she find her former room intact? Would she find the pictures of Jesus hanging on the walls like they used to? Would the analog clock be silently running? Or would everything be different? Of course, it would be different.

Their house guard had set his eyes on everything that her parents owned, or perhaps it was their neighbor. Their politically famous and businessman new neighbor. Cursed be that day. The 7th of April. The day the hopelessness began. While thinking about it, Anne thought about it and realized that it didn't actually start that day. Her parents had occasionally taken them to a place called Kinyinya around Deutsche Welle; they'd stay there for a couple of days and come back. There were days that her parents talked about leaving Rwanda, and they never truly did.

Right there, in the car back to the ruins, she realized that the killings hadn't struck overnight. They had been planned meticulously; they weren't a spontaneous disaster; they had been well prepared. Given that the killers seemed to be normal people who lived with them day to day, how would they have had the guns, machetes, and cubs? How would the entire country just wake up and start killing each other over a plane crash?

It was never an impromptu thing. There had been deliberate killings. The kind that was going to alter her life forever.

Chapter 8

Nobody suffers once. Life is all about that. But what does one make out of the suffering that is stuck inside the soul for a long time? Anne was now a 15-year-old girl, tall and regal like her mother, not skinny or plumb but curved in all the right places, with rounded hips and an afro that resembled her late father's.

She had learned to get along with Aunt Costa's children, two girls and one boy. The boy was rarely home, as he studied in Uganda at Makerere University. Anne had no idea what he was majoring in, only that it was related to business. Their entire family was into business, except for her, who wanted to go into science. It would be a few more years before she would choose "section," or the combination she would do in A level.

Diane was 18 years old and a student in high school at one of the good day schools.

Lycée De Kigali (LDK) and Matilde was 17 years old who also went to the same school. They were older and in secondary school. Their conversations and stories that they shared were always entertaining.

Anne wouldn't say that anyone would ever think she was just a cousin, not Aunt Costa's child. It was as if she was her own mother. Aunt Costa had made sure to be where her parents could have been. She had raised her as a true Christian, as her parents had been. She was tender but firm with her. She talked to her about all the things she needed to know. One time, they'd had a conversation about her teenagehood after she had gotten her first period at 13.

They were sitting in the master bedroom, large with green walls, a picture of Christ next to Mother Mary's, and a cross.

"I understand your confusion, but it's entirely normal for girls to have blood flow during some days of the month." Aunt Costa had said with a chuckle.

"Yes, Matilde told me about it." Anne responded in a matter-of-fact tone.

"Don't be shy or anything; if your mother were here, she'd tell you about it, and I have decided to be both your father and mother for the time being." Aunt Costa said with misty eyes.

Anne was always amazed at how her aunt was such an emotional person up close, but a ruthless businesswoman from afar.

"Yes, I appreciate that."

"So, here is what you will be using during these times." Aunt Costa reached for a pack of pads and opened it.

She took an underwear and started demonstrating to"Thanks, Anne how she would do it. When she was done, she handed it to her.

"I know Matilde might have shown you how to do it or might have done it for you, but this is the way it is done. I want to be the one who shows you!"

"Thanks," Anne said without meeting her aunt's eyes. While she found it nice, she was also shy about discussing such delicate matters with her aunt.

"There are things you should keep in mind. You should know that you're fully a woman now. It means that if you sleep with a man or a boy, there are chances to get pregnant. I understand that you might like someone, but if you find yourself in a difficult position, ask me questions. I will answer." Aunt Costa continued.

"Are you saying that I would only get pregnant if I slept with a man during my periods?" Anne asked, curiosity getting the best of her despite the fact that she wasn't meaning to ask such a silly question.

"No, that's not what I meant!" Aunt Costa laughed. "I meant to say that within a woman's month, there are phases of low, high, and moderate chances of getting pregnant, and the period is when the unused eggs flow out of the body. I don't have better ways to explain it, but not just on your period; it can be at any time of the month."

"Oh okay,"

"You should just try to track if your period comes regularly or irregularly, like at the same dates or not, and the days your flow lasts. Also, hygiene is very important. Keep your private parts properly cleaned with clean water. I hope it helps. Back in the day, our mothers taught us at a very young age, mostly because we spent longer with our parents than we do now. These days, as parents, we are trying to find employment, work for money, and see whether we can feed you, get you clothing, school fees, and other essentials."

Anne processed the information slowly, and she was thankful that at least her aunt was talking to her about it now. She didn't think of her as a too-young girl who shouldn't know grown up people's business. As usual, she was frank about the realities of life.

"Thank you so much, aunt, I will keep that in mind." Anne responded.

"I have been trying to persuade you; you can call me mother; I would prefer it that way. All of you are my children now. Despite the fact that I am not your biological mother, I am still your mother." Aunt Costa pleaded.

"Okay Mama,"

"Oh, I almost forgot one thing, a very important thing." Aunt Costa said, "It's not unusual to have feelings for boys at your age or when you get a bit older. However, of all the times, if you ever find it hard to resist a boy when you grow up, make sure to use protection such as condoms. I don't want to show you now, but always remember to have protected sex or abstain until you are married. It is what is befitting a Christian and virtuous girl like you." Aunt Costa said.

With that intimate conversation they had, Anne still refrained from sharing that she wasn't a stranger to the animosity of men in heat for sex. They would not stop at anything. One person she had trusted to protect her had done the unspeakable for her. She felt dirty to this day. She hated herself for the shame and cowardice of not talking about it. He not only got away with his actions, but he even got paid for keeping her safe.

Even now, Anne recalled the conversation with her aunt. It was good to know those things. Only that, she had no confidence in herself as a woman. With all the stories that Diane and Matilde brought from their school, Anne thought that indeed, that kind of conversation was necessary.

Matilde was only 17 years old, but she had a new boyfriend every other month, she had new crushes every other week, and she wasn't even ashamed of talking about it with Anne. It was only in front of their mother and brother that Matilde and Diane didn't recount their boyfriend stories.

Anne felt blessed to have been raised with the three of them. Their brother, Claver, was almost like the man of the house because Aunt Costa had no husband. He was much older, about 25, and always had forward-going plans. Anne wondered whether her brother would have grown up into such men as well. She had never met them afterwards.

The family dynamics were just too good. Her classmates always talked about fearing their fathers and mothers; they talked about how their families never really had much conversation. It was as if their parents were too strict and would only beat them up if they tried to bring up any kind of story. At Aunt Costa's dinner, it was storytime. Matilde and Diane were gossiping about their classmates, and Aunt Costa was talking about the clients she had met during the day. It was only Anne who seemed not to be able to share any stories.

Today, she found out that she would go to a good secondary school, led by priests—a perfect school, as Aunt Costa said. They were now going to have a celebratory dinner at home.

Their house maid had cooked pilau rice, meat, and french fries; a vegetable salad and fruits were also served with her aunt's favorite bottle of wine. Everyone would be home, including all of her cousins and their aunt as well.

"Wow! You're such a brilliant kid! Congratulations on getting into Groupe Scolaire de Butare!" Claver cheered when he entered the room. Anne smiled shyly. It was going to be a night full of praise for her. For some reason, Matilde and Diane were never at the top of their class as she was, but it didn't seem to bother them at all.

"Eh, if you saw the way she was preparing for the national examination, you'd think she was going to do the world's exam instead!" Matilde jested.

"Well, that's why she's going to a good school, though!" Diane countered.

"Sha, everyone has their own thing; I swear, I would never want to go to a boarding school; even in day school, I am always in trouble with the authorities. Imagine if now I was in a boarding school!" Matilde said.

"Well, we actually need to talk about that, Mati; your marks got even worse last term! You'll be lucky if they let you pass." Claver said, sipping on his glass of Primus.

"Aha, she's just saying this because Mama is not home yet; if she were here, she wouldn't brag about her trouble at school." Diane said, sitting down next to Claver. "By the way, Clave, when are you really coming back home for good, or is Uganda just enough for you now?"

"Don't change the subject, Dia; whether mother is here or not, it's necessary to at least have some good marks. I get it that you guys don't want to do sciences like Anne, but seriously, good marks are good for getting jobs." Claver retorted sternly.

"Come on, we already know that. I actually think that maybe I am having issues with the teachers, so they lower my marks." Matilde complained.

"Or you're busy reading novels and going for 'agasobanuye' instead of getting back to your studies." Diane said.

"My God, a kettle calling a pot black. We are the same. Aren't we always together?" Matilde rattled.

"Well, my marks didn't get lower; yours did." Diane responded.

"Neither of you is doing anything right. Besides, you're taking the focus off our star of the night! Anne has made us proud, sha. I will drink to that kabisa." Claver said.

"Heeee, Dia, I forgot to tell you something. Do you know that Keza was dumped last night by the way? I swear, the way she and that boy were going, they would get married right after school. Apu, it was all lies." Matilde said.

"You're lying, Keza? With all that beauty and the way she acts so important, did she get dumped? You can't be serious." Diane said and high-fived with Matilde on it. Apparently they share a common envy for Keza, who was their rich kid classmate.

Like true siblings, Matilde and Diane were on each other's throats one minute, and the next, they would be chummies. Anne had a free subscription to their drama.

A few minutes of banter passed before Aunt Costa arrived. She handed her always-heavy purse to Anne, who rushed to the master bedroom to keep it. After all, she was the youngest girl in the house, and Matilde and Diane were never interested in being at their mother's disposal like she was.

"So, I heard you got into Groupe Officiel; that's great news for sure. I am very happy about it. Finally, you're going to be a big girl, alone at boarding school. Unlike those who like furniture in this house, staying at home even through school." Aunt Costa said, looking at her daughters.

"But Ma, what's wrong with going to day school?" Matilde asked, and as usual, her mother didn't respond; she just continued with what she was saying. Anne came back to the dinner table.

"Well, eat well, Anne; there's only a few weeks remaining. I have put together your school fees; Matilde and Diane will take you shopping for the requirements. Aha, schools these days ask for things; it's like you're going to get married or something. Anyway, we'll find them!" Aunt Costa said.

"Can we eat, though? I am hungry!" Matilde made a face at her brother, who shook her head and laughed. She was just an impatient character, and Anne wondered whether it was her character as a person or whether it was an attitude budding from being the last born.

**

The day of school came earlier than Anne had expected. She had been very anxious about leaving the home that she was accustomed to. She was an introverted person who rarely talked to anyone else other than her cousins. Aunt Costa had tried her best to make her be more interested in socializing, taking her to different gatherings where people had baptism parties, weddings, and more, but to no avail.

Now, she would have to socialize with the students in her class. It wasn't an exciting thought for her, but it had to be done. Aunt Costa and Diane were to accompany Anne to school. They had one of Aunt Costa's drivers take them from Kigali to Butare on a three-hour journey. They had stopped to buy snacks along the way, and Diane was telling Anne to eat as much as she could because she would not be eating them in a long time.

Upon getting to school, they went through all the necessary procedures, got her a uniform that fit her, and got her a room in the dormitories.

The school was mostly brick buildings that looked quite old, and the pathways to the classes and the dormitories were well-swiped dirt roads, very characteristic of Catholic schools. After getting everything into place, Aunt Costa and Diane had to go back home.

"So, Anne, keep the advice I gave you close to your heart. I will leave you some money for you to use when in need, but avoid wanting extravagant things. I believe I have packed you everything that the school mentioned you would need here. This is a school of excellence with many bright students, but do your best to bring good marks. Other than that, pray to Mother Mary and her son, Christ; everything will go well." Aunt Costa lectured as Diane stood there, amused.

"I understand, mama." Anne agreed.

"Don't just listen to Ma; she's telling you the necessary stuff. Have fun and make new friends, okay? Don't remain that shy; otherwise, you will suffer at the hands of the bullies." Diane added.

"But, Dia, is it true that there are too many bullies?" Anne asked, worried.

"You're about to find out; you will tell us at the end of the term!" Diane laughed.

"She's lying; they're just normal students. Don't let her make you worried; everything will be fine!" Aunt Costa reassured Anne.

They both hugged with double kisses on the cheeks, like how they were raised, in a French manner, and left.

Anne was left alone as she watched her aunt and cousin leave. For the first time, she looked around her. Different people were in one space, families leaving in crowds through the small gate, as children were left there. Many seemed to make friends and leave together hand in hand, while she was alone, looking like she was lost on a new planet.

Indeed, it was a new planet. New surroundings and new dynamics. She headed to the dorm, all the way surveying the space. She sat on her neatly made bed and started packing notebooks, pens, and all the school supplies into the school bag. She was nearly done when another girl, slightly her age, appeared. Sweat beads had formed on her nose, and she was looking like she had made it a few minutes before the closing of the gates.

"Hey, I am so late; they almost closed the gates on me. I should have gotten tickets for an earlier time." The girl said and shook Anne's hand.

"Urgh, now I have to sleep on an upper bunk bed, just above you! Do you think we can exchange?" The girl grunted. Anne looked at her wordlessly.

"What do you mean?" Anne asked.

"I am asking, can we exchange the beds? I sleep down, then you sleep up." The girl explained. "My name is Rosine, and I am in my second year here. Sometimes I get issues because climbing up the bed is hard for me."

Well, you should have come earlier, Anne thought, rolling her eyes in her brain. However, for some reason, she had taken a liking to Rosine.

"Okay." Anne responded. "But I was already done with making my bed, so you'll have to help me redo it on the upper bed."

"Oh God! You're such a nice girl. Thanks, no problem; let me just help you right now. Soon it will be time for dinner, so we have to hurry." Rosine said, dumping the bags she had down and getting started with the duty.

"So tell me, you look like you just came into the school, am I right? Or you changed schools from another one?" Rosine inquired.

She's clearly going to talk my ears off, Anne thought.

"I just joined the school. It's my first time in boarding school." Anne responded, "My cousin says there are lots of bullies here."

"Well, she didn't lie, but it's not that scary. Most of the time, if you are trying to be too cool, that's when they prey on you mostly." Rosine responded.

"Eh, is that so? I am afraid then I will be an easy target because I don't speak much, and I hate to be bossed around as long as I know that I am doing what I am supposed to do." Anne explained.

"Worry not, you've given me your spot on the bed. I will try to spend time with you and help you make friends with my classmates, so they will protect you if anyone tries to bully you." Rosine said. They all finished their preparations and headed to the dining hall.

Newcomers were recognized and told about the rules of the school and the schedule they should follow.

Rosine kept her end of the bargain by being by Anne's side. They did most of the things together, going to the chapel, the refectory, and every other event.

However, Rosine was the talking piece among the two of them. Anne was mostly thinking about her classes.

Anne was mostly thankful to Rosine because she kept her secrets safe. She had nightmares. In which she talked and sometimes screamed. Rosine had convinced everyone that it was her instead of Anne.

One fateful night after they had an event related to the commemoration of the 1994 Genocide against the Tutsi, people shared testimonies, and students also shared theirs, which triggered many students. Anne managed to hold it in, but she had a nightmare. She was running with Donatha, and men with machetes were hunting them. In other parts, she was fighting against Jean. The surprising part was that the dream ended when she, herself, was trying to run after men to kill them. She murmured in her sleep, "I will kill you; I will finish your entire people. Please leave me alone. Let me go."

Rosine awoke her with soft pats. "Anne, Anne, wake up; you're talking in your sleep!"

Anne woke up panting and traumatized, and she asked Rosine about what she was saying.

"You were saying really bad things. You were asking the person to leave you. You said you wanted to finish them. Is it because of the testimonies we heard earlier?" Rosine asked in a whisper to not awaken other girls in the dorm. Anne, embarrassed by her own nightmare, shook her head.

"I don't know why; I have had nightmares for some time now. I haven't found my parents and brothers, and the men who ran after us during genocide always appear in my dreams." Anne said.

"I understand; please go to sleep. We'll try to find a way to solve this. We will talk about this tomorrow. It's Saturday tomorrow." Rosine reassured her, and they both went back to sleep.

That night, Anne never went back to sleep; the memories kept flashing in front of her eyes, mixed with the images of the testimonies people had shared earlier. Wondering how she could find peace within herself, tears stained her bed sheets until dawn broke. She wondered whether to play it cool and hide her sorrow or whether to just spill more of her secrets to Rosine.

Chapter 9

Saturday morning went as usual; the girls and boys were cleaning the school compounds, halls, and classes. Because Anne and Rosine were not in the same year, their assigned cleaning locations were different. Anne spent the majority of the morning keeping to herself as usual, cleaning with her classmates without talking much. While the majority of the students had been affected by the genocide, many of them studied under the FARG (Fonds d'assistance aux rescapés du génocide), and many of them had episodes here and there due to the tragic things they had seen. They talked about the normal daily things of the new life they were leading now. Some of them had their parents or uncles in jail for the atrocities they had committed, which made them ashamed of their lives.

Anne tried to not engage with anyone. Oftentimes, she would be lost in thought, staring into nothingness, her mind wandering into the things that were not there. By the time her peers would ask her things, she would be lost in the conversations. Girls, just like Aunt Costa's daughters, talked about the boys they fancied, and they gossiped about who was with whom. Anne was rarely engaged in those conversations. The only ones she would entertain were Rosine's stories. She had a way of capturing her short-span attention; she wouldn't ramble on without making sure that she was following. She tried to also keep her away from the bullies at school who teased her about her absentmindedness.

After lunch, Rosine and Anne went to wash their clothes together. As they finished setting up everything to get ready to wash, Rosine started with her stories.

"Guess what? I just found out that Clarise in my class is dating a guy in a new cohort; he is in {insert combinaison}! Who knew that even Margret would find someone? The girls say she's not that pretty, and the guy is from a wealthy family." Rosine started.

"Your classmates are mean; Clarise is a good person!" Anne exclaimed.

"No, c'mon, we both know she doesn't compete with the likes of Nyiramushonganono, but anyway, I am not even talking about being pretty or anything; just overall, there are better girls than Clarise." Rosine rebutted.

"So are you saying she doesn't deserve to be liked by a nice guy or that she doesn't deserve the best in life?" Anne asked, point blank.

"That's not what I'm saying; I'm trying to make you see how the guy had other choices. I mean, every girl was flirting with him, washing his dishes, and all that stuff. They tried to sit with him during the mass as well. Clarise wasn't even trying at all. She always acts mighty, by the way; every single time, she behaves like she's the better person of all of us." Rosine said with a bitter tone.

"Okay, why do I feel like maybe you also wanted the guy for yourself?" Anne chuckled.

"I don't want any guys at all. I was just saying there are other girls who deserve a guy like him. Have you seen the type of cars his relatives drive during school visits? That family is wealthy;

they probably even have some who live abroad and send them loads of money." Rosine said it with an excited tone.

"What I'm hearing right now is that maybe you also had a crush on that guy. It's not bad to like someone, but it's also okay for the other person not to choose you." Anne said. "Besides, didn't you say there is a guy who courts you during the holidays? Just settle with that one."

"Ah, don't even mention that one. Didn't I tell you that his uncles were tried during Gacaca and they were guilty? Plus, my mother would probably kill me if she found out that I kept seeing him after she told me not to talk to him." Rosine said sadly.

"I get that; we all have pasts, but you can't dwell on that. His uncles are not him. He didn't commit any crimes. He is probably also ashamed of what his family did." Anne reasoned.

"Ugh, don't convince me. I liked him in the first couple of months when he started courting me, but again, other than having managed to make money as a businessman, he only finished primary school. My mother wouldn't accept our relationship anyway. I just don't want to even think about it." Rosine said. "Anyway, enough of the boys. These clothes won't wash themselves; I need to finish washing them before the sun is down or the best spots are taken."

Anne mumbled in agreement under her breath, and the two girls washed their clothes. Hanging theirs in what Rosine had called the best spots. In an hour, they were done with washing and cleaning their shoes.

When they were back in their bunk beds, Anne busied herself with shining the shoes that they would wear next week while Rosine folded clothes and bantered with the other girls in the dorm.

However, the peace didn't last long. Rosine pressed the issue that Anne had hoped the other girl had forgotten.

"So, ready to talk about last night? It's not going away. We better talk about it now or never." Rosine said.

"We don't have to talk about what happened last night; I don't think anyone heard me, so we can also let it go and pretend it never happened." Anne evaded.

"I need you to realize I am not trying to breach your privacy. You should realize that I am your friend who's willing to listen to you about whatever." Rosine reassured her.

"So, as a good friend, aren't you supposed to let me be for now until I feel comfortable to share?" Anne questioned.

"For the entirety of our friendship I have let you hide. I do the majority of the talking, I sometimes tell random stories hoping you'd find them hilarious or relatable enough to share, but you don't. I feel like It's my right to actually dig deeper this time." Rosine said, sounding genuinely concerned. Her brows knit together as if she were trying to hold back the tears.

"Well, I understand. I am sorry if I am sometimes overbearing to you or burdensome. It's not my intention to do so." Anne apologized.

"Then let's talk about it." Rosine urged Anne.

"We can't talk about personal stuff here, though, can we? These girls would be listening to our secrets and all of that. Which I obviously don't want to do. They run their mouths like a sport." Anne suggested.

"Let me put on some clothes, then we can stroll around instead of sitting here. It's not a good idea, as you said." Rosine agreed.

The two of them got up from the bed and went on a stroll. The dirt pathways in the school were now very clean and free from any people roaming around, just the two of them. A Saturday afternoon had always been like that: students getting their school garments ready, boys playing football, and girls sitting on some greenery, but mostly the pathways would be empty.

As they strolled, none of them began; they only walked in silence for about five minutes, each hesitating on where to start their difficult conversation down the memory lane. It was an exercise in opening individual wounds that haven't been scarred yet. It was almost as fresh as if it happened yesterday, even though the tragedy was years behind them now.

"I don't want to start the conversation like I always do, but I won't push you too far to the edge either. You can tell me whatever information you want to tell me. My mother tells me that talking relieves grief." Rosine said, sounding wittyer than her usual self.

"I will go first. It's okay. You don't always have to cover up for my shortcomings Rosine." Anne said, cleared her throat and began her story.

"My parents loved each other deeply, and they loved us too. We weren't really poor or anything like that. We went to good schools and had great neighbors. We went to church very often too." Anne started.

"Hmm."

"When Genocide happened, I was about eight years old. Our house guard was the one who attacked us. He came with men with machetes and tried to take what we owned. However, it didn't go well for him. Another influential Hutu man came and took my parents at that time. They had to leave me behind with our housemaid."

"You guys had house guards and maids! I only heard that from people who lived in Kigali." Rosine exclaimed. "I would assume you guys could have paid to stay alive!"

"We lived in Kigali, somewhere called Gatsata. My father tried to give money to the guy to hide us, but it was in vain. When I was left with Donatha, the housemaid, the house guard tried to rape her so she had to act fast. She took the little money my mother had given her and we fled. We would be running for days, we saw people cut other people's heads off and they would throw them in the river." Anne stopped abruptly and breathed in heavily keeping the demons at bay.

"I can imagine. Donatha was a good person! She could have left by herself. You were the only child at your house? You're lucky." Rosine said.

"No, I am the only girl in my family, but my brothers had been sent to Ruhengeri to stay with one of my aunts who lived there. Unfortunately, my parents thought it would be fine in a couple of days, but instead people started to kill each other aggressively instead. Apparently, Donatha knew where my grandparents on my mother's side lived so we fled there via a car of someone she'd paid." Anne narrated.

"It must be God who was protecting you, I heard some people were burnt alive in cars when they tried to escape or some would be dragged out to be killed by the roadside before they reached where they hoped to hide." Rosine commented.

"Yes, it was God only, we managed to arrive where my grandparents lived, but they were killed in front of us the next day by one of their neighbors who wanted to loot what they had. From there, my memory is foggy, but I do remember that Donatha persisted as much as she could, telling people that if they could keep me alive, they would be paid when the war was over. Luckily, there was a man who had liked her, he's the one who helped me to reach my aunt, Aunt Costa, when FPR finally chased away the perpetrators in the south." Anne finished.

"What happened to Donatha? She didn't come with you when you met Aunt Costa." Rosine queried.

"Well, she didn't. I wished she would come with us, but she also had to start looking for any of her surviving relatives, if there were any at all. I don't know if it was Aunt Costa who didn't want to bring her with us or if she willingly didn't want to come with us." Anne confessed.

"That's so sad. Someone saved you, and you weren't able to stay with them after these hard times." Rosine said sadly. "So what's exactly the cause of your nightmares and absentmindedness? Most of the time we talk, it's like you're not there at all."

"I don't know really; was it watching people kill each other? Or if it was because I would be locked in some dark rooms to survive? I really don't know. It's these things that come into my mind. Being raped at the house of the man who was also paid to keep me safe may be one of the reasons. I've spent long periods of time feeling very worthless."

"What? He raped you, and he was paid to release you as well? Unbelievable!" Rosine screeched.

"You're probably the first person I have told this to. I was feeling ashamed and worthless that it wouldn't turn back time. Talking about it wouldn't make me go back to who I was before that happened anyway. With the way that my father loved me and treated me like a little princess, I couldn't deal with what the man had done to me." Anne's eyes got misty.

"I am so sorry this happened to you. Now I understand why you were crying that you would kill that person and asking the person to let you go in your nightmare." Rosine mumbled.

"Don't tell anyone any of this. It's just a secret that I am sharing with you. Even Aunt Costa has no idea what happened then. She tries her best to educate me and tell me a lot of things; if I told her that I was raped, she would be more heartbroken than she is now." Anne said, a tear rolling down her face.

"I am so sorry about that. It was as if at that time people were possessed by some sort of demon." Rosine mused.

"So, what's your story? You promised you would share how you managed to escape." Anne chuckled, feeling embarrassed that she had bared her soul in front of a stranger like that.

"My story is a bit different from yours, of course. I wasn't being targeted, but sometimes they wanted to kill us because we were not participating in the killing. My mother was my father's second wife, and I am the only child. Other siblings are way older and from another woman. It was difficult for us to be honest because we wanted to hide people who were running away from my father and other men who were killing, as well as their sons. My father would come to our house daily to find anyone who had hid there. Sometimes we would hide people inside the pits where we fermented our beer, but after awhile, my father discovered that the place existed and people would be there. He found one young man there, and he said he would kill us in front of us so that we would never hide anyone ever again. My mother only tried to divert attention; for some, it worked, but for others, it didn't. My father actually confessed and gave himself up when they started to lock up the perpetrators. I have never visited him in prison, and I think the memory of him will fade away after a while. I don't think I want to see that face of a monster who calls himself my father."

Rosine shared, looking ashamed of her father's sins.

"Rosine, you and your mother are innocent like everyone else. I have learned to blame people for their own actions. My father used to teach me that I should be accountable for my own actions. He used to say that it is me who has the power to choose between doing good things and bad things. My mother was a bit more fierce, so she would say, The one who commits sin is the one who should bear the punishment." Anne empathized.

"Each time I dread going to the holidays, my entire village is full of people whose families were murdered, slaughtered, or shot by my father. That's why my mother doesn't want me to be involved with the other guy. She says she has had enough of monsters already."

Rosine said.

"I understand. Just take it slow; as you said to me earlier, talking relieves grief. Thanks for listening to me; now I feel a bit lighter. Finally, someone sees me for who I am after a very long time. You've been a good friend to me." Anne said, pulling Rosine into a hug.

Rosine was taken aback by Anne's sudden show of affection, but she appreciated the sisterhood they shared. Despite their stark differences, they had managed to be each other's refuge and safe space.

"Thank you for helping me get over this too. Whenever I share my story, many people look at me like it's me who committed all these murders that my father committed, but you accepted me more easily than I thought you would." Rosine appreciated.

"The only problem is that you will be gone very soon; just another year, then you will shift to another school." Anne lamented.

"No, I don't have to change schools; I can study harder so that I can come back here; there is my combination of choice anyway." Rosine said with a shrug. "It's also near my home even though I choose to be a boarding student."

"Really? Let's promise to come back here, the both of us!" Anne said with excitement that she hadn't felt in a very long time. With a pinky swear, they sealed their sisterhood.

Anne wondered what would happen if she pursued more healing opportunities; what if she could also be open to joining different groups? Maybe sharing indeed was more relieving than she thought it would be. However, would other people be as understanding as Rosine was?

Maybe it was time to start asking about what had become of her brothers and parents again. She decided that she would mention it to Aunt Costa to see what could come out of it.

After their heart-to-heart, Rosine started with a high-pitched voice that signaled mystery.

"You can't believe what happened earlier in my class," Rosine said.

"I hope it's not another story of who is dating who!" Anne sighed.

"No, it's way more interesting. It's still Clarise, actually! I can't believe I didn't start with that particular story."

"Are you going to tell me the story finally or not?" Anne laughed.

"Wait, I need to take my time. So, it was in class a bit before we discovered that she got into the relationship. The teacher literally beat her up, and she had a crisis due to the trauma she has. The girls said she was almost hospitalized, but her parents told her to come back to school. That's how she captured the attention of that guy. He's such a handsome but really sympathetic person. Ahaa, I wish it was really me." Rosine said.

"What? I can't believe you. The guy is just a good person! And, I was right, you had a crush on him. Don't be jealous; your match will arrive one day." Anne said, patting her friend's shoulder.

Despite her own words, Anne wasn't very convinced of her own words. She wasn't thinking that there would be a time she would get over her past and think that she could be interesting to anyone.

Part 3: Restoration

Chapter 10

2 years later...

Just as they'd promised each other, Anne and Rosine went back to the same school. Contrary to what many of their colleagues claimed—that the school was way too restricting and not a happy place to spend six years of education—they both didn't mind. What mattered for them was to be together again. Thank God, it indeed happened.

Over the two years, Anne and Rosine had started to participate in community work, supporting the survivors. They joined the association that had been created to bring together the survivors or those who had been heavily affected by the genocide years prior.

However, the biggest change they'd achieved together was finding their way into a deeply godly lifestyle again.

They were devoted Catholics who served at the altar a couple of times a week, sang in the choir together, and participated in other groups like Communauté de l'Emmanuel. Anne was happier to reconnect with God; her life was a bit smoother, but she had yet to get the courage to share her entire truth with Aunt Costa.

Every other holiday, her aunt tried her best to make her feel like a part of the family, took her to family reunions with the extended family, and introduced her to neighbors, just like a mother would. It actually almost felt like she was more of Aunt Costa's daughter than just a regular niece. She fit in where her father and mother could have been. Aunt Costa also went to greater lengths to be supportive. She had even become conversant with Rosine during the visiting days; she would also offer Rosine rides on the closing days. This only solidified the bond between Anne and Rosine.

It was the first day of the new school year. Anne was moving to the A level of secondary school, and Rosine was in the second year of the A level. They were happy to reconnect after spending the long holidays apart, only calling each other once or twice during that time.

All the students were gathered in the refectory having their first meal of the school year, talking, and waiting on the school administration to pass the announcement of the opening of the school year. They had a lot to catch up on. However, their conversation was interrupted by the sight of someone Anne hadn't seen in a very long time. Jeph.

Jeph, her old childhood friend whom she had liked as a young girl. Jeph, whose parents moved away just before the Genocide. How could he be here?

"Rosi, remember my other friend? I told you we lost touch when I was young, just before the Genocide?" Anne whispered.

"What? Where did you see him? Show me, which one is he?" Rosine asked with excitement.

"He's seated on the table behind us, the third boy on that table; he's the light-skinned one with a watch on his wrist." Anne said, and Rosine's head whopped to see who that was. "I didn't tell you to look!"

"I have to see for myself! He looks like a rich kid. Didn't you say they went abroad? How do you know he's the one, though? What if it's someone they look alike?" Rosine cautioned.

"I can't forget how he looks. I am very sure he is the one!" Anne exclaimed.

"So, do you want to go and greet him to at least confirm who he is?" Rosine queried.

"Do you think it would look nice for me to go out there and ask an almost-near stranger whether he remembers me or not?" Anne rebuked.

"Well, look at it my way, and you will realize that you actually aren't strangers as much as you think you are; it's all in your head. If you can recognize him, I bet he can recognize you too. Plus, you two have a lot to catch up on!" Rosine remarked.

"I get what you're trying to do, but it won't work, trust me. I am not the kind of person who will make the first move. I will wait for him to reach out. If he does remember me at all." Anne said.

Rosine decided to drop the case. It was Anne's first year in biochimie, she had always had a knack for sciences, even though her aunt had advocated for her to do things related to languages so she would take over the business and operate in different countries. She had never heard of anyone else in their family who had been in sciences, which was a popular choice for many parents to urge their children to do.

That evening, the school administrators flooded the dining hall as the school principal gave a speech. He welcomed new students, extended a special mention to those who had been at the school at their lower level, and chose to come back to the school again. He talked to them about how the school had and would always be a school of excellence; therefore, for it to keep the reputation, they had to uphold virtuous characters as it is in the school norms.

All the while, Anne tried her best not to whip her head back and watch Jeph, who was seated behind; however, the entire time she could feel someone's eyes fixated on her. Only that, she couldn't make out if it was him or someone else.

After the long speech, a ripple of applause went through the dining hall, reflecting the excitement of the new students who couldn't wait to experience the school and ascertain the renowned excellence the school had amongst other schools and the general public.

"You're looking so bothered. You're lucky there are no after-dinner preps today; otherwise, you wouldn't be doing it at all." Rosine said.

"I should be laughing at you. For us, we just came; as for you, you might even have a pop quiz from that complex senior five biology teacher!" Anne mocked.

"Well, jokes on him because I had nothing much to do over the holiday; he can ask me anything he wants about senior four biology, and I will respond to them!" Rosine boasted.

"Ahaa! We shall see. I think the principal is done; let's just go to the dorm. I am feeling sleepy, and there are still some of the things I need to unpack and organize. I don't want to start this semester in a disorganized mood." Anne said.

"Okay fine. Let's go then." Rosine agreed.

＊

The next morning, Rosine and Anne went through the rituals of the school as they usually did. Waking up at 4:30 am before many other people woke, bathed, made their beds, got dressed for the morning designated chores, then went for morning prayers.

The school obviously had a quite rigid schedule that no one was allowed to defy, but there would always be a couple of students who thought too highly of themselves to comply with every single detail. Anne and Rosine were obviously not among those. Very often, going against the flow of a river hurts the person opposing it, not the river. Therefore, they liked to think of the schedule as a tool to help them, and they did their best to go with that flow.

During the mandatory morning assembly, Anne was standing alone because this was the time when people stood according to their years, so she couldn't be with Rosine. All of a sudden, she saw the figure from behind. Jeph. Even as a child, she could still notice his build from anywhere.

She breathed in and hoped he wouldn't turn around. They sang the national anthem, the monitor gave the announcements, and all the students headed to their classes.

The block for the A level was different from the O level. Rosine rushed through the swarm of other students and found Anne so they could walk to the classes together.

"Hey, finally we're on the same block. You used to go the other way; now you're moving with the older people. Congratulations." Rosine jested.

"I don't know whether that's a compliment or an insult." Anne said it with a smile tugging at her lips.

"Trust me, it is both! If I don't bully you on your first day, I will be labeled a very bad friend." Rosine said. "Did you see your childhood friend again?"

Just as Rosine said that, Jeph passed by them in a rush, trying to overtake the other students who were walking a bit slower, including the two of them.

"Jeez, what if he heard us?" Anne said.

"You're acting so out of character these days, you know! Anyone can be your childhood friend! Besides, with the way he's walking as if he's the one who'll be teaching the class, I don't think he had time to eavesdrop on random conversations." Rosine sighed.

"Okay, fine, you have a point there."

"I am always right. You're in denial." Rosine said.

They both reached the two-story brick building. The school, despite being one of the oldest in the country, still had the building standing where very minimal repairs had been done. The buildings were not dilapidated, but they no longer had their old glory especially after the tragic genocide which had led to ruins of many things.

The senior four classes were downstairs while the senior five classes were upstairs, therefore, that meant that Anne reached her class before Rosine did. They said their goodbyes as if they wouldn't be just meeting for the break in a couple of hours.

Anne entered her class, and there Jeph was seated in front alone. It was very ironic because he was seated on the first row of the middle column with his height. Standing at 1.85m, with broad shoulders and a lean torso, he definitely looked like he'd become a basketball player or a volleyball player, one of the two. Yet, he was seated there like it was the most rightful thing to do.

"Hi, do you remember me?" Anne said abruptly, which took Jeph's attention from organizing notebooks to her face instead.

"Hi, did we meet last night or any other time before today? I honestly don't remember. I am very new to the school. I am not among the people who returned. Are you?" Jeph asked, looking a bit embarrassed that he couldn't remember who she was.

"Well, I used to go to this school before, and I came back because I wanted to do biochimie." Anne confirmed. "It's not what I meant with the question, though. We used to be neighbors back in the day, before the Genocide.. However, right before it happened, they mentioned that you guys had moved abroad or something."

"Wait, you are joking! I can't believe it; now we are meeting! I remember you, Anne! We used to hang out sometimes! Our families were friends. It's so nice to see you again." Jeph beamed at her, extending his arm for another handshake.

"I thought you wouldn't remember me, though!" Anne said in relief that he actually remembered her.

"How could I forget? You're probably the only surviving person I have reconnected with from my childhood. Remember the other children who lived near us instead? They actually were all murdered, the likes of Remy, Kayiranga, and others." Jeph said, and his smile disappeared.

"I can imagine; we were all dispersed here and there trying to stay alive, so it's unfortunate that they didn't make it alive." Annie said woefully.

Before they could go down the memory lane, other students started to come in. Anne remembered that she hadn't claimed a seat yet.

"Anyway, we'll talk. I have to get a place to sit!" Anne said.

She was a bit relieved that she had found someone from her childhood, but for some reason, she felt uneasy about being in the same class. She wondered why her heart was racing all of a sudden. This was an uncalled-for sentiment. She was older now, and so was he. She had been negatively affected by the genocide; he hadn't. It was a dynamic she didn't want to explore.

Before she could wander off into her own thoughts, the teacher disrupted things in the class and told everyone to sit according to the seating plan he had created randomly. They positioned Anne and Jeph across from each other. He was put at the far back of the middle column, while she sat in the middle of the left row near the door.

Wow, why would this happen? Basically, all the times I try to move my head, he'll be seated within my eyesight. Anne thought, gnawing her teeth.

The entire day, Anne was in a bitter mood and less chatty with her only friend, Rosine. She would only nod or smile at what Rosine would say. It was when they were moving from the dining hall for dinner that Rosine finally asked her what was wrong.

"I don't know what your problem is now; just talk to me if you need to. Did you get your period? That's the only time you're very bitter. At least the first three days." Rosine said, her tone concerned.

"I actually don't have any problems at all. I just don't have anything to talk about." Anne said blankly.

"Come on, you can literally fool everyone else except me. I know you don't speak much to other people, but when it's me, you literally tell me everything, down to the smallest details that I don't even think you noticed." Rosine reasoned. Still, Anne didn't budge.

"Okay, fine, I will tell you. We're in the same class." Anne finally said.

"You and who?" Rosine asked, her brows frowning in confusion.

"Jeph!"

"Eh, isn't that supposed to actually make you happy?" Rosine asked.

"You don't get it. I think I might develop feelings for him." Anne admitted. Rosine laughed so hard at the sentence that teardrops formed on the corners of her eyes, and her knees went weak.

"Why are you even laughing? Is that funny?"

"Yes, it is!" Rosine said, gathering herself. "You know, for a person who's been laughing at people with crushes or those in relationships, you have lost your mind completely. You saw that guy last night after ten years, and you're already having feelings for him." Rosine said.

"It's not a big deal. Having feelings is a common thing. Anyone can have them." Anne defended herself.

"Really, I thought amorous feelings feared you or something!" Rosine said, earning a side-eyed glare from her friend. "Alright, look here; I think these are not feelings, to be honest. You're just happy that you saw the guy again after so long. Or maybe this is because he feels like a familiar figure from your past."

"I know what I am feeling, and it's neither of what you have described. Anyway, let's not even talk about it or anything. I'll probably get over it soon.

The only pity was that she didn't get over it. Instead, she sought all opportunities to be closer to Jeph. He was astonishingly good at physics, so she would find random topics that he understood well. They would spend more than their normal preps. He would sacrifice his weekends to explain the concepts to her as well. Anne was no longer glued to Rosine's side during different activities. She'd instead sit close to Jeph, comment on things he found interesting, and listen to conversations about sports just so she could be in his vicinity. Occasionally, Rosine would swallow her pride and hang out with the two of them. However, it seemed as though Jeph enjoyed her company more.

Their conversations wouldn't be pretentious or boring; Anne would be watching the two of them talk about volleyball and how the two of them had played for their school teams very often. They would talk about old French songs, most of which Anne didn't know about.

One Saturday, when they were doing laundry, Rosine brought up the topic.

"By the way, Jeph sounds very mature and interesting! Remember the other day when we talked about the novels we had read? We both read the same titles!" Rosine remarked. Anne continued to wash the clothes aggressively without a response.

"Hey!" Rosine called her out when Anne didn't respond.

"What? Oh, sorry, I didn't hear you. What were you saying again?" Anne asked. *I heard what I didn't want to hear.* She thought to herself.

"These days, you seem a bit off. What exactly is the problem?" Rosine asked, concerned for her friend.

"I have no problem. Maybe it's the new year that's kicking in. Nothing much, to be honest." Anne said.

"Soon enough, it'll be the visiting day; your aunt will come. I am sure maybe you can trust her more with your problems than you are with me." Rosine pointed it out bitterly.

"What does that even mean?"

"I mean, it's been months since this academic year opened. You're already starting to be so distant from me. I guess I was only important to you when you were not at the A level yourself." Rosine mused sadly.

"Why would you even think of me that way? You're the closest person in my life. We have been keeping each other's secrets for years now!" Anne refuted.

"I know you said you had feelings for Jeph, and I actually think he and I can be friends even though he's a bit behind. In terms of age, he's older anyway. I think you're bothered by the fact that we seem to have some things in common." Rosine said.

"That's not the case at all; you can be friends with whoever you like, and I already told you that I am trying to get over him. This absolutely has nothing to do with you. I just feel a bit weary, that's all. Maybe I need to pray harder than I do currently. God will make everything okay. His will shall be fulfilled." Anne said.

Fortunately, her ruse to redirect the conversation worked.

"Yes, God's will is everything and beyond in this life. I assure you, we'll be fine, and never hesitate to talk to me if you feel like some things are not right between us." Rosine reassured her friend.

Anne prayed in her heart that she would not let mere feelings for an old childhood friend separate her from a friend who'd been with her through thick and thin, offering the solace she needed when she was facing her demons.

Chapter 11

The visiting day came earlier than Anne had expected. This was a very anticipated day, especially for young students in the lower secondary. The majority of those in the A level were used to spending time in the canteen and eating other foods that the school didn't offer, like donuts, biscuits, chapatis, and more.

Aunt Costa had always been committed to making Anne feel loved, so she followed all the visiting days religiously. She didn't have to open her shop on Sundays anyway; she'd go to pray the second mass. However, on days where she needed to visit her at school, she'd rise earlier to attend the first mass. The driver would probably have been notified weeks ahead. She usually marked important dates on the calendar in their living room.

Anne was, however, surprised that even her stubborn cousins were in tow along with another unfamiliar guy. The new guy looked to be somewhere around Cousin Claver's age, 25, and his name was Lionel Kabarisa. After the basic introduction, they found a small shade in the garden and sat there.

"So how are you holding up in your combination of choices?" Matilde asked before everyone else, trying to rub in that Anne had chosen a scientific combination for her A level.

"Not even asking her how she's doing, you're going to choose that! My dear child, you're very stubborn." Aunt Costa said.

"I know she will never understand why I chose this; many other students are here because their parents or guardians want them to do all of these hard combinations. She has a little bit of a point there." Anne attested.

"People come before all these other things. We should just thank God that we're all alive first. Let's first say, Our Father and three Hail Mary's." Aunt Costa said.

Anne closed her eyes as they all said the prayers silently, then Aunt Costa said an extra short prayer. She had a feeling that something was not right. She just didn't know what it could be.

In over ten years of living with her aunt and cousins, they rarely had issues. Usually, it would be normal business challenges that her aunt tackled adeptly without much back and forth. She was just as good as her father had been.

It was moments like these that Anne reflected back and wondered what it could have been like if her parents had been alive. Now the memories and questions had started to flood her mind incessantly. Where were her parents and brothers? If they were dead, where were their bodies? If they were alive, where did they live?

The prayer ended, and Anne confessed to God in her heart that her mind had been elsewhere and not on the prayer.

"So, yes, tell us, how are you? You are used to the school already, so how are the lessons now?" Aunt Costa asked humorlessly. Something was amiss; she wasn't her usual bubbly self.

"All is well; I am actually doing well; so far, nothing is going wrong. I don't regret my choice so far." Anne responded. "You should tell me the news outside there instead; for us, there are not many exciting things going on, to be honest."

"Well, we don't have much good news either this time." Diane said her face was void of expression.

"Eh, what happened? Aren't you getting married soon? Or did you dump him?" Anne said with a laugh, and when no one laughed with her, she clamped a hand on her mouth.

"Well, my dear child, the wedding is still on, but we probably might have to postpone it. We thought we'd get permission for you to attend it; instead, you'll be going to a funeral." Aunt Costa said.

"What happened?" Anne asked, her voice quivering. "Who passed?"

"Well, the past doesn't want us to rest at all. You're right, some people passed on, apparently a very long time ago, and we are only finding bodies now! Ahaa." Aunt Costa said.

"None of you is actually saying what happened." Anne said, her voice rising. "Who passed? Whose funeral are we attending?"

"Your parents. They've been found. Dead, in the backyard of your neighbors' house." Aunt Costa said.

No one dared to move a muscle at that moment. Anne looked shattered, her eyes brimming with tears that didn't fall. She'd never been able to cry during such hard times.

"Do you want me to give you space to talk?" Lionel, who'd been silent the entire time, spoke.

"Why would you do that? You're family as well. You knew my brother as well, didn't you? You were younger then, but still, you knew him. Whoever dared to kill him is a monster. Gasana could never hurt a fly! Why did people have to be that cruel?" Aunt Costa said. "His dear wife, a fierce woman, strong in spirit and flesh! All this time, I was hoping I would meet them again! I would tell them how I missed them! How their child has blossomed into this beautiful woman!" Aunt Costa sobbed.

Diane pulled out a small handkerchief and handed it to her mother.

"I am sorry about the crying; it's not the time nor the place to do so! I should be strong for you, Anne! I am sorry." Aunt Costa said.

"I understand." Anne responded. "When is the funeral? We can talk about it later on."

Lionel stared at Anne, his face frowning at the storm of a girl in front of him. In most cases, a person receiving this kind of information would break down, regardless of the place. However, her face was just ashen, void of expression.

"Anne, this is not a good time to talk about this; you're right. We still have to wait and hear from the authorities about when we can have the bodies. It should take a week. Then we will have to decide about the cemetery or just wait to bury them alongside other bodies that have been found in the area. Apparently, the man who killed them and buried them in his backyard had other people do the same in their house. They kidnapped people with money, and if they couldn't find enough loot from them, they would end up killing them." Aunt Costa rambled on.

"I am not sure I want to talk about this now. Maybe you can try to ask for permission from the authorities. At least they can be put to rest very soon." Anne said.

Matilde and Diane looked at each other with suspicion. Lionel tried to reach for Anne's hand, but she shifted her body. It was as if she were a feeble, broken glass wall that would crumble at the slightest touch.

Aunt Costa headed for the offices as Anne went to the dormitory to pack a couple of notebooks and clothes she'd taken in a small backpack.

All the way to the dorm, she could barely think straight about where she was going. Her mind was filled with memories of her dear parents. The smiles, the times they used to dine together as a family—the last time she saw her mother telling her that she'd come back, which she never did. She silently prayed for strength.

She tried to find the positive in the situation; she at least now knew that her parents had been received into heaven with Mother Mary and Jesus. She would no longer wait for them to emerge out of the blue, to appear from thin air, just like she lost them. She would say to pray for their souls to rest in peace.

Luckily, getting permission from the school authorities went off without a hitch, and in a few minutes, they were on the road back home. The entire ride was silent. It was as if no one wanted to talk about anything. Everyone, lost in their own thoughts, listened to the car revving through the dirt roads, then back onto the tarmac. Only the driver would comment on the traffic when another driver committed a foul.

When they were back home, Aunt Costa's housemaid had prepared herbal milk tea made of ginger, lemongrass, rosemary, and thyme. They sat around the dining table, drinking it, when Aunt Costa decided to talk about the entire affair.

"Anne, we probably forgot to properly tell you about Lionel; he's working for me now; he's the son of the man back at Deutsche Welle, where your father used to take you to hide. I am not sure if you remember him from there. His father was a distant cousin of ours; Lionel was trying to look for jobs, so I offered him one. Since he used to live too far, I also allowed him to stay in Claver's room so that he would get to work easily. I am getting old anyway." Aunt Costa explained.

"Thanks again; job searching can be hard these days. I thank you for the trust." Lionel smiled shyly, his gaze on Anne.

What is he even looking at? Anne thought to herself. *Nothing is funny or amusing!*

"Anne, do you want to eat a banana or something? There is some bread as well." Matilda said, ever so clueless about how to console grieving people.

"No, I think I am full on this tea already." She responded.

"You'll eat dinner, right? They cooked your favorite food." Diane prodded.

"Yes, don't you miss some home-cooked food after all that food from school?" Lionel added.

"She'll eat something, obviously." Aunt Costa affirmed.

"Does it look like I am starving to death for you? My parents are not eating now, are they? They're dead and rotting all because of greedy men. I hope they are haunted by the lives they took for the entirety of their lives." Anne burst out, shedding a single tear, her throat tightening and her jaw clenched.

She realized the hurt in her aunt's eyes and swallowed the last part of the outburst.

"He is behind bars. The murderer of your parents. He was the one who confessed where he put the bodies. He killed his own wife first because she had been wanting to let them go. After he killed her, he found them and killed them. He says he regrets what he did. He shouldn't have done it and other lame explanations that perpetrators forge." Aunt Costa explained bitterly.

"Of course, we're victims; we have no choice but to live with the consequences of their actions while they enjoy living." Anne said.

"Anne, I know how you're feeling; it's always difficult to be alone without your immediate family. Trust me, I know the feeling. Mine were killed in front of my eyes. I am only lucky I survived, but for my own sake, I must forgive and relieve my heart. Hate is heavier than grief." Lionel soothed.

Anne got up and headed for her room.

She was out of words. She was out of emotions to feel at this certain moment. She was grateful that she had a family that loved her and took care of her, but grief from the past was too heavy. She just wanted to sleep off her pain.

That night, she dreamt of her mother singing to her, then her father taking her to the first mass. She dreamt of her brothers playing football in their front yard. She dreamt of Donatha's resistance to the wannabe killers.

The following days were just multiple times back and forth with the authorities, planning how they would relocate the body to a cemetery. Anne was given a choice for what they would do as the living daughter of the deceased. On the day of the funeral, friends and extended family showed up in masses. Everyone had good things to say about her parents. His business partners and even rivals showed up with praise. She only hoped that she would grow to have a heart like her father's and strength like her mother's.

Laid next to each other, just as they loved one another, her parents were finally raised to the ground with the respect they deserved. She thought she'd have strength by the time she was handed the time to speak, but she still found words stuck in her throat.

"I love you, and I always will. You've made me who I am today. I will try to carry on your legacy of integrity and bravery, as you both were. I miss you so much, no matter how many years pass. I miss you, ma, and I miss you, pa. I wish you were here today. I have managed to get into scientific class, as I always dreamed of doing so. I hope you will be in heaven, smiling down at me. I hope God will rest your souls in heaven as you deserve. I am alone without the wonderful brothers I had, but I will try to be as strong, brilliant, and successful as you would have wanted me to be." Anne spoke.

Ripples of sobs went through the crowd, with the stronger ones handing handkerchiefs to the ones crying. Anne didn't shed a tear.

Back home, Anne sat on the porch alone in the dark. Until a figure approached and sat next to him. She recognized his frame. It was Lionel.

"Hey, how are you feeling?" He asked softly. "Would you like something to drink, like water or soda?"

That was the last straw. Anne broke down. The glass finally shattered. The pain that had piled up over the years exploded. She cried, her body heaving with each scream that she tried to swallow to not make noise.

Lionel did not speak; he simply approached her cautiously and hugged her. Sometimes, people don't need sympathy; maybe they need a presence. A tranquil witness to their misery. Someone should gracefully hold the space for them.

After minutes of crying, Lionel's t-shirt was damp with her tears. Suddenly aware that she was crying in the arms of a stranger, Anne pulled away and wrapped her arms around her slender frame.

"I am sorry about that. I don't know what came over me." She apologized.

"It's only human. Maybe you've kept this pain to yourself for a very long time. When I found my parent's bodies again after the Genocide, I was the same way. I'd seen them get ambushed when I ran from the murderers, but pain is pain. It's meant to be felt. The only people who should be ashamed of their tears are the murderers, not you." Lionel said softly.

For some reason, Lionel seemed like a good person. In the few hours she'd seen him around, he'd been helping, offering to do one thing or another for anyone. He'd been going around with handkerchiefs at the funeral. At the house, he would not sit still; he'd be serving drinks to the guests. Now here he was.

"Why are you here?" Anne asked. "I mean outside. I just wanted some fresh air."

"I also wanted some fresh air. Humans need air to live." He responded, and Anne smiled through the sobs at his witty response.

"I am serious. You don't even know me." Anne said.

"It doesn't matter. The fact that I don't know you is very irrelevant. Everyone needs a shoulder to cry on. I think you're not very comfortable with showing emotions. You like to keep things to yourself. I know there is God in heaven whom we should cast our burdens to, but people were also made in His image; we can share pain." Lionel said.

Maybe he's right; I have been holding onto this pain for too long. Anne mused.

"Can I ask you a question?" Lionel asked.

"What question would you possibly ask me at this time? My aunt must have told you everything already. She tells everyone my story even when they don't ask." Anne said. "She seems to trust you already; she even employed you."

"How old were you during the 1994 Genocide against Tutsi?" He asked solemnly.

"I was eight years old." She responded.

"How did you get separated from your family, then?" Lionel asked. "I mean, you don't have to talk about it if you don't want to."

For an unfathomable reason, Anne wanted to. She wanted to relive everything from the beginning; she wanted to sit with her pain. Even the story she had only vowed to tell Rosine, she divulged. It was the most painful of her memories. She told him of the nightmares she had occasionally. She told him about Rosine; she even told him about how she was now struggling with the friendship because they both liked Jeph.

"Do you think it's selfishness?" Anne asked.

"What's selfish?"

"To start hating Rosine because we both like Jeph? She's been a great friend for all these years since I started high school." She said softly.

"Do you really like Jeph? Or is it because he's a familiar person from your past?" Lionel asked.

"Rosine asked me the same question." Anne responded with a chuckle. "Honestly, I don't know. He is familiar; I liked him when I was younger as well. I don't know, maybe I am at that age where people want to be liked and wanted. I don't think if anyone knew my past, they would like me. I am no longer a virgin anyway. That was taken away from me."

"Well, I can't say that I understand that feeling. Virginity is important to women, maybe. I believe that whoever loves you truly should be able to oversee your hurtful past. They should focus on the strong woman you will become and the beautiful, kind-hearted person you are now." Lionel reassured her.

"I think..." In mid-sentence, Anne heard her aunt calling for her.

"She's calling you now. Go listen to why she's calling. I'll be out here for a bit longer." Lionel said, helping her up from the steps where she sat.

"Thanks again for listening." She flashed him a smile in the dark.

Epilogue

Things can fall into place gradually. Holding onto the weight of the past can shadow your present and your future. Anne went back to school, and every single time she would reminisce on her past, she would hear Lionel's words echo in the depths of her heart.

Before the first semester, during the 'shomage', she spent more time praying and joining different groups. She started making friends in her class as well. Her face, which was mostly clouded by a lack of expression, would be lit with stories and curiosity.

"I need to know what you ate during the time you went home. The way you've changed is astonishing. One can barely notice that it's you." Rosine commented as they swept the roads one day.

"What do you mean?" Anne laughed.

"You know what I mean." Rosine side-eyed her. "You smile more and listen more. I thought a funeral was meant to make you more somber than merry."

"You wouldn't understand. I think I was kind of able to answer at least some of the questions I had in mind. I finally put my late parents to rest, and I also had an eye-opening experience. I have learned that holding the grief in my daily life affects me more than it helps me." Anne explained.

"You've even become philosophical." Rosine clapped at her.

"I didn't! I learned that God, who allowed me to survive, has a plan for me. I should not worry about the future. I just need to study harder so that my parents in heaven will be proud of me." She affirmed.

"Speaking of studying,. I have some news for you." Rosine said, her eyes brightening in excitement.

"Kagire inkuru! I can't wait. You haven't been giving me any good gossip these days!" Anne said, relishing the story.

"Jeph asked me to be his girlfriend." Rosine said, dropping her broom.

"Wow! You guys are a good match. I am happy for you. Now I see why you've been acting strange and avoiding my class. So, did you accept?" Anne asked.

"No, I didn't."

"Why didn't you?" Anne exclaimed.

"Because of you!" Rosine responded. "It's not appropriate. You knew him first; you guys grew up together. You have feelings for him, and I don't want to stand in your way. Besides, he's behind me in education. It's inappropriate."

"You are joking!" Anne laughed. "I know we met first, and I was just having the hots because of the age and need I had to be seen and wanted by someone. I thought about it and realized that you're more suited for him than I am. He's always been a good person; he helps me to study as well. However, it's not more than that."

"Are you sure?"

"No, are you sure? Are you sure you want to give him up? I can't lose a friendship—a sister I have found in you—over a guy. I haven't found romantic love, but I am loved by other people in my life. If it feels right to you, then do it." Anne advised.

"There you go, giving me life advice while I am older than you!" Rosine laughed nervously. "I mean, scholarly romantic relationships usually don't last, but I enjoy it when I meet up with Jeph just to talk about different things."

"That's between the two of you. If you don't try things out, how will you know if they will or will not last?" Anne asked. "People can love each other for years; true love will always prevail."

"I need to seriously understand what you have eaten!" Rosine remarked. "You're a changed woman. Prayers, charity work, ahaa, you've really been touched by the Holy Spirit of the Lord."

"Well, helping others makes me happy. I think I want to be a pediatrician in the future. I want to help children." Anne thought out loud.

"I can't believe we're even talking about life dreams right now; you're still in senior four! Do you know how many years it takes to become a doctor? Or even the marks it takes to be admitted into medical school?" Rosine challenged.

"I know there are many years, but I have a dream. I will not rest until I have achieved it." Anne said.

"What about marriage? Many people get married after high school and get that education when they're already married. What about your own children? Don't you dream of them as well?" Rosine asked.

"I mean, as you already said, I am just in high school now, so my focus is to study. I am sure I will one day become a mother, or a doctor. For now, I will do what I can." Anne responded, her voice calm and peaceful. "Now, I want to know, are you going to say yes to Jeph?"

"I am also focused on studies." Rosine said sarcastically, rolling her eyes.

"We both know you want to be in a relationship, though!" Anne said.

"I mean, I will be done with school when he's still studying. I want to be in a relationship with someone who will be ready to marry when I am done with school." Rosine said. "Obviously, Jeph is academically driven; he will pursue education abroad. What will I be doing at that time? I can't wait for the seven years he will study medicine like you."

"Well, I wish I had an answer to your questions. Maybe you should pray about it; God might guide you through all of these hardships." Anne concluded.

The rest of their high school years, Anne spent her time supporting other students who had trauma from the Genocide, using some of her supplies to help those who would come without enough of the supplies. When Rosine graduated, they both cried because they would not be spending their time together all the time as they used to. Rosine would go back to the countryside where her mother lived, and Anne would study and go back to the city. They promised each other to keep in touch, send each other letters, and call whenever possible.

They upheld their promises.

When she graduated high school, Aunt Costa held a party for Anne. Their extended family was invited, as were neighbors, church friends, and some of the students, including Rosine, who had to travel from Butare to Kigali to come to the party.

After all the eating and dancing, Aunt Costa asked for a speech.

"Thank you all for coming to celebrate my daughter's graduation." She started. "After my brother and his family went missing during the Genocide, I had no hope of ever finding anyone. Fortunately, I found Anne. She's my niece turned daughter. She has been a wonderful child, a brilliant girl whose future is as bright as the sun! I am very sure my brother and his family are very proud of where they are in heaven. Anne has looked beyond the hardships, discovering the bodies of her late parents, the persistent disappearance of her brothers, and other traumatic experiences. She has shown that she is brave and ready to go very far in life. Once again, let's toast to her continued success and her kind heart."

Everyone cheered and clapped for that.

Ku buzima bwacu! Ripples of happiness echoed through the crowd.

One certain person who'd been busy the entire night making sure the drinks were in full supply finally got to talk to Anne alone when many of the guests had left.

"You've finally graduated high school. I have no doubt you'll get a presidential scholarship. You really worked hard for it. Sometimes I wondered how you would manage to study at night during the holidays." Lionel said.

"I have a dream, and I have to work for it." Anne replied.

"Yes, you have been working for it! Now you can rest."

"It's now that it's actually starting. Medical school is going to be harder than high school." Anne disagreed. "Regardless, you have really helped me go through a very difficult moment."

"Ahaa, if you can do it, please do it! I have already dedicated my life to business." Lionel laughed. "On a serious note, I want to talk to you about something."

"What could that be?" Anne asked, her brows frowning in surprise.

"Can we go outside?" He asked. They both walked out to the porch. Cool air chilled them a little bit.

"So tell me, what did you want to talk about all of a sudden?" Anne persisted.

Lionel cleared his throat as if he were very nervous. Anne knew him as a strong guy who handled other people's issues like a pro. He loved people and his job. It was evident that he was a people person because the clients had almost tripled since he started working at her aunt's shop.

"I want to ask you a question that has lingered on my mind for a couple of years now." Lionel started. "I know we met when you were facing hard issues; you opened up for me when I didn't expect it. You managed to see beyond your own trauma and got involved in charity, both at school and at the church."

"I am still trying to understand what you are getting at!" Anne laughed. Their porch, which now also had electricity, set the perfect scene. The light illuminated her smooth, chocolate skin, and her eyes lit up.

"Be easy on me!" Lionel chuckled. "What I am trying to say is that I already know that you're kind and resilient. Here at home, you're the only one who takes turns cooking and cleaning; spend time with the housemaid as well."

"I was actually saved by our housemaid, Donatha; I wish to meet her again. They are also human beings who deserve to have company and rest sometimes." Anne mused.

"I know; I wish to meet that kind woman who allowed God to use her to save you! Your smile, your laugh, your kindness, your beauty—all of it has blinded me to other girls. I meet many women and girls at the shop, but even when you are at school, I look forward to the visiting days. I have fallen in love with you;

can you ever find it in your heart to return that love?" Lionel asked finally.

Anne looked away shyly. She couldn't say she'd never thought about him during the times she was at school. Ever since the conversation they had, he was always on her mind. During any triggering moments, she would remember his words.

"No, I won't allow you to avoid me. I know it is hard for girls to admit that they love someone; I won't force an answer out of you either, but please at least look at me." Lionel said.

He reached out for her hand and turned her towards him. Finally, Anne spoke. Her voice was thick and down an octave.

"I can't say I've never thought about you or noticed you. I am grateful for your presence in my life." She said, "No one has ever told me those words, so I don't know how to respond to them."

"You can't even say these words." Lionel said. "But I want to hear you say it. Just the key word, love."

"It's hard; I am not used to it." Anne said, trying to pry her hands from his, but he held on tighter.

"I know it's new to you, but can you try it for my sake? I have been in love with you for almost three years." Lionel said.

"Three years? You know how to hide things, then." She said.

"You know the most ironic thing: everyone in this house teases me about you; they all know I fell for you a very long time ago. It's only you who didn't know." Lionel chuckled. "Can I hug you? I miss your hugs sometimes. Whenever you hug me, it would be one armed hug like I am a hot saucepan or something."

Anne laughed out loud at his comment, but she granted his wish. They hugged as if they had never done so before.

It wasn't a scary feeling. It was a pleasant and peaceful feeling. She felt a wave of calmness wash over her. This wasn't the type of love that is dropped on you; Lionel didn't mention he loved her for one particular thing. He had taken his time to learn her traits, learn what motivated her, learn who she really was, and listen to her story intently and attentively.

At this moment, she felt wanted and appreciated. She didn't feel the need to hide or grieve. Lionel wasn't an exceptionally handsome guy who would turn heads in the streets; he wasn't wealthy, just on his journey to build himself, but he was a brave man who was willing to put in the work and trust in God to bless the work of his hands. He was genuinely interesting and interested in her.

When he finally released her, he still held her hand, looking at her face dotingly.

"So, will I get an answer today or should we go back inside? If your aunt or cousins saw me holding you like I was, I wouldn't hear the end of it." Lionel said.

"I don't think I can just answer right away that I want to be with you, but you're so easy to love. Lionel, you're a genuine person, and I am thankful for your presence in my life. Just give me time to think about it. So far, I don't think my response will be an unpleasant one. I think I can fall in love with you too." Anne spoke softly, taking her time to articulate her feelings.

"You can't imagine the relief you've brought to me today." Lionel sighed. "I honestly wasn't confident you would be interested in a guy like me. A guy who hasn't gone to a prestigious school like you did and who doesn't even have dreams to do so. Anne, all you should know is that I support your dreams. I have waited for you for three years. I can wait a little longer if that is what you need."

"Thank you so much. It means a lot to me." Anne responded.

That night, Anne lay in bed and replayed her entire life as if it were a book she was reading. She discerned that every day is an opportunity God gives to rewrite one's story.

At some point, the country was full of streams of blood; the next, people struggled to forgive and others to confess, but now it was time to start healing.

She realized that she still had no idea where her brothers were, whether alive or deceased. However, she had at least put her parents to rest. She had seen her grandparents and other people get murdered; she had been raped, but she was alive. She was not aware of where Donatha was, but she hoped she was harvesting the fruits of her kindness. She'd been under no obligation to save her employer's child, but she still risked her life for it. Many people had become completely orphaned, alone in the entire world, but she had her aunt, cousins, and other extended family members.

Anne reflected on the friendships she had in her life with Rosine, Jeph, and Lionel. Wonderful people whom she had been blessed to meet. She prayed God would give her a long life to support others as she had been supported. She hoped she would live to see her home country develop and move on beyond the scars that adorned the citizens. She wanted to live in a united Rwanda, and she was looking at herself as a stepping stone for that.

The future was not certain, but her commitment was. She would trust in God and do her best.

Scars are badges of resilience; grief is the proof of life; and present actions are the vision of what the future can be. Everyone deserves healing, love, and appreciation.

Thank you for completing *Revival*.

We would love if you could help by posting a review at your book retailer and on the PageMaster Publishing site. It only takes a minute and it would really help others by giving them an idea of your experience.

Thanks

Elise Micomyiza on the PageMaster store
https://pagemasterpublishing.ca/by/elise-micomyiza/

To order more copies of this book, find books by other Canadian authors, or make inquiries about publishing your own book, contact PageMaster at:

PageMaster Publication Services Inc.
11340-120 Street, Edmonton, AB T5G 0W5
books@pagemaster.ca
780-425-9303

catalogue and e-commerce store
PageMasterPublishing.ca/Shop